D1002081

Delete This At Your Peril

Also by Neil Forsyth

Other People's Money – The Rise and Fall of Britain's Most Audacious Fraudster (with Elliot Castro)

Delete This At Your Peril

One Man's Hilarious Exchanges with Internet Spammers

Bob Servant

Skyhorse Publishing

www.skyhorsepublishing.com

Library of Congress Cataloging-in-Publication Data is available on file

ISBN-10: 1-60239-275-7
ISBN-13: 978-1-60239-275-5

10 9 8 7 6 5 4 3 2 1

Design by Roger Hammond
Printed in China

Contents

For my brother Alan. And for the lion, that most magnificent of beasts. But mostly for Alan. Thanks.

Introduction:
Meet Bob Servant

I remember the first time I saw Bob Servant very well. It was in the late 1980s and I was a ten-year-old cycling through Broughty Ferry when I saw a burger van opening for business down at the harbour. This was a novel event both for me and, it would turn out, for Broughty Ferry and I skilfully reined in my Raleigh Burner and watched the momentous scene unfold.

There were a couple of glum-looking men sprucing the van up, switching on ovens and so on, but my attention was drawn to another man who sat on a nearby bench watching them and occasionally offering words of advice that appeared to go largely unheeded.

I can really remember only a few details. One is that Bob had a bright red face, another is that he was drinking what I thought at the time was a milkshake but I now strongly suspect was a cocktail, and the final thing I can remember was what he said. He said, with an epic sense of despair, 'Fuck me Frank, watch the fucking sausages.'

The next time I saw Bob was perhaps five years later when I opened my bedroom curtains and there he was at the other side. The suddenness of my appearance caught him unawares and for a moment Bob threatened to fall off his ladder but he caught himself and gripped the window frame, panting and sweating and saying, 'Christ, you nearly fucking did for me there son.'

Bob, it seemed, had taken over the window-cleaning round that included our house. I can recall my Mum's confusion at the increased frequency of the window-cleaning team's appearance. 'Someone's making a bloody fortune,' my Dad used to summarise when he returned from work to hear of yet another visit.

Bob and I quickly became not friends, but certainly firm associates. For a bored schoolboy, Bob was a man of the world who advised with little encouragement on anything from women to feverish speculation on local thefts, and his ongoing feud with a local newspaper. For Bob, I was a willing listener and the search for willing listeners has probably been the great cause of Bob's life.

In the winter Bob would appear on Saturday mornings, scaling his ladder dressed for Kilimanjaro rather than our two-storey home. I would crack open the frosted glass and it would begin. Both he and I would be going independently to watch Dundee United in the afternoon and, from deep within his array of padding, Bob would offer a range of optimistic predictions as steam rose from his bucket and multiple layers.

In the summer, Bob would curl a thick arm over the windowsill and start, usually with:

'Ah, how you doing? I was just saying to Frank there...'

And then he would unleash a story, a joke or, often, a plan. Bob's plans were extraordinary, containing an audacious mixture of ambition and completely undiluted self-belief. He toyed for a long time with entering local politics for what he called a clean-up campaign. That plan was quietly abandoned when Bob and Frank, who he had appointed his election agent, could not decide on a suitable slogan.

Frank, I should point out, was Bob's regular window-cleaning sidekick and, I presumed (correctly), the original Frank from the burger van. Sometimes there would be other men with Bob, all of whose grave moods would clash markedly with his, but Frank was the standard. Perhaps because of this sustained exposure to Bob's peculiarities, Frank's depressive air was almost overpowering.

While Bob was halfway into my bedroom explaining how he was going to build a private zoo, or complete the Dawson Park monkey bars course in less than a minute, or swim the River Tay once things warmed up a bit, I would peek down to Frank, who would be standing at the foot of Bob's ladder.

At the very best he would look crushingly bored. At worst I would sometimes catch him staring at Bob's ladder with a distant look in his eyes, as if calculating just how many of life's worries would vanish with a hefty kick.

It was a few years on, when my friends and I began sneaking into Broughty Ferry's bars, that I saw a different side to Bob. His window-cleaning operation had been passed to strangers but his message on the matter was very clear.

'Not to worry,' he told me with an elaborate wink, along with the much-repeated suggestion that he had landed a significant windfall on the round to go with the riches from his years as the owner of a cheeseburger van.

There was also something about gypsies stealing his ladders that always sounded to me like a botched insurance job. Once, emboldened by drink, I put forward that theory to Bob, who replied with a quote from Winston Churchill that bore no relation to the situation whatsoever.

It became strange to walk into a Broughty Ferry pub and for Bob not to be there. If the place were quiet he would be hunched over a barstool, lecturing the barman and jabbing a finger to make his point. In busier pubs he would retreat with companions to a table, though this didn't stop the barman being generously incorporated by Bob into his conversation.

He had an eclectic collection of associates who you will soon discover are in his thoughts to this day. There was a uniformed security guard, a local lawyer who had been struck off and a group of traffic wardens who I'm sure were supposed to be working at the time. But more often than not, Bob's immediate company would be drawn from any combination of three men.

There was a small, sharp-faced man known as Tommy Peanuts who wore a suit with loosened tie, which did not seem to halt daytime excursions through the pubs of Broughty Ferry. He was quick with the cutting remark and often this would be aimed at an unknowing Bob's expense. I would feel a strange pang of shared betrayal when Tommy slipped in some mockery and Bob laughed innocently away.

Chappy Williams and Bob were locked in a love-hate relationship that clearly still rumbles along. The two should be brothers, such is the inherent rivalry as they compete for social standing in the bars of Broughty Ferry. This battle is generally waged through incredibly intricate practical jokes often taking days, if not weeks, in planning and execution.

And then there was, and is, Frank. A man referred to by Bob with, I believe, genuine fondness as Frank The Plank. As I gained increased access to Frank's company I realised very quickly that he wavers spectacularly on the very edge of sanity. Much of this is undoubtedly due to living next door to Bob. Whatever warped scheme or activity Bob is indulging in, you never have to look far to find Frank.

So that, for me, was Bob Servant. I moved away from Dundee, and a highlight of any return would be a chance meeting with Bob, for whom nothing ever really changed except the steady flow of ideas. He toyed for a long time about opening a café, only to give up in fury when someone else did the same. He started another clean-up campaign which started and finished with him shopping a corrupt member of the local Limbo Walking Club to local press. He declared to myself and other astonished drinkers that he was going to buy a pair of ostriches and mate them in his garden (he never did).

But away from thwarted dreams, Bob had been doing something else. It was something that no one knew about and it was when I became the first person to be told that the relationship between Bob and myself changed forever.

* * *

As I sat reading a newspaper in a Broughty Ferry bar of an evening in early 2007, a familiar combination of reddened forehead and bunnet appeared above the page. It was Bob and he wanted to talk, but there was something different about him. There was none of his usual grandstanding and he employed a nervous whisper, darting his eyes around the pub in fear.

He confirmed that I was a writer and then slipped into a muddled explanation of some strange pursuit he had undertaken after winning a computer in a raffle at the local bowling club. He talked of Africans and Russians, of emails and computers, and hinted at long nights of cheap wine and Internet exchanges.

'I mean,' he said with a sly grin, 'They're chancers, these people, Neil, real cowboys, but we've had some fun.'

Intrigued, I accepted Bob's invitation to learn more. We walked through the darkened streets in near silence, with Bob occasionally attempting further description only to give up in frustration or an extended bout of laughter. To be perfectly honest, I was a little nervous. Bob's eccentricity was all very well in public but, on the way to his house with him babbling about lions and rubber belts, it was slightly disturbing.

My alarm increased when we arrived at Bob's home. Although an impressive sight from outside, the interior was a study in chaos. There were collections of empty bottles throughout, various pieces of fancy dress hung from doorframes and an extraordinary number of novelty duvet sets. After we weaved through to the living room Bob directed me to a computer that he activated and went to get us drinks.

As the computer warmed up I noticed some scraps of paper beside the keyboard with scribbled notes. Amongst the jottings were names with arrows connecting to startling terms. 'Lanzhou', for example, pointed to 'rubber belts', which in turn pointed to 'stuff Clive's mouth with prawn crackers'. Bob returned with the drinks and brought up an email account on the screen.

'That's it,' he said simply and retired to a couch on which he lay in silent contemplation as I made my first entry into a very different world. An hour or two later I turned back to him.

'Bob?' I asked, 'Would you be interested in writing a book?'

Neil Forsyth and Bob Servant (right), Broughty Ferry, summer 2007

Editor's Note:
An Overview of Spam

I should probably offer just a little more guidance. The email exchanges that Bob enters into in this book are with a variety of the Internet's less worthy inhabitants that fall roughly into three categories of criminal intent.

The 419

This scam is an update on old-school advance fee fraud in which the aim is to con someone into paying a small advance to enable the transfer back of a massively greater sum. Named after the article of the Nigerian criminal code that refers to the crime, it usually takes the form of an unsolicited email suggesting that there is a ludicrous amount of hard cash in Africa looking for a private transfer to a willing individual's bank account.

The money will usually be described as being held in a bank or security company and the legacy of a recently deceased monarch, politician or military leader. Their relatives will need to sneak the money from the country but first bank details will be needed, the more the better, and eventually some form of deposit paid. In 2006, a report by a research group concluded that Nigerian scams cost the UK economy £150 million, with the average victim losing £31,000.

Local Agents Needed

A less colourful attempt to gather bank details from those tempted by the promise of imminent riches. In this case, the approach is the suggestion that an individual or company needs someone on the ground to receive payments for them, remove a percentage, and pass on the balance. Often the email will claim to be from a company or individual in the UK. This is because the vast majority of spam is designed for North America and it's obviously felt that the British background adds credibility. The true aim is to gather bank details, while those who use this scam could conceivably be based anywhere in the world. The cases in this book include the cover stories of a Chinese company and a British painter.

Fake Russian Brides

As it sounds. The spam (and photos) claims to be from a Russian bombshell who throws herself with admirable dedication into the exchange, soon professing her love for the entranced chap at the other end. What happens next tends to be one of three things. The first is that after a number of largely generic emails from the Russian woman (who in actual fact may be neither Russian nor a woman), a false agency will appear on the scene asking for a fee for the communication to continue. Sometimes this is done quite professionally, with a fake website offered as evidence.

The second variant, as happens to Bob, is for the Russian woman to audaciously suggest that she makes a visit to her new friend's country. Money for tickets and a visa are the only thing that stand in the way of married bliss.

Finally, there is the sudden arrival on to the scene of a dying relative, with cash for medicine needed at some haste. The Internet is awash with embittered accounts of these methods and some surprising cases. In 2004, for example, a Californian man was convicted of impersonating Russian women and stealing more than $1 million from over 300 men worldwide.

* * *

So that's the background to how the various propositions are first presented to Bob in his bulging spam collection, before the exchanges quickly deviate from the norm. Bob tried to engage some other spammers – fake Viagra merchants and fraudulent share tipsters for example – but these emails tend to be computer-generated.

For the purposes of this book and with the emails being genuine messages sent by the criminally minded, the vast majority of the editing has been the removal of identifying factors.

Bob, I must add, has been less than helpful with the process of editing his vast exchanges that often ran for weeks, if not months. He seemed to find it a great source of amusement that I had to spend, for example, two days trawling local radio transcripts to see if he had indeed suggested live on air that he often wipes his bottom with newspaper. As a result, I have occasionally offered clarification when I think it is needed. Mostly, I think it is quite clear that Bob is being less than honest with the frustrated, and somewhat bewildered, crooks.

Each man is a hero and an oracle to somebody, and to that person whatever he says has an enhanced value.

Ralph Waldo Emerson (1803-82)

The thing is Xiong, you're over there in China and I'm here in Broughty Ferry. But you're just a man and I'm just a man. That's what I'm saying. We're all just men. Apart from women.

Bob Servant (1945-)

1
Lions, Gold and Confusion

From: Jack Thompson
To: Bob Servant
Subject: Delete This At Your Peril

FROM HIS ROYAL HIGHNEST, JACK THOMPSON

Dear sir,
Permit me to inform you of my desire of going into business. I got your name and contact from the chamber of commerce and industry. I am JACK THOMPSON, the only son of late King Arawi of tribal land. My father was a very wealthy traditional ruler, poisoned to death by his rivals in the traditional tussle about royalties and related matters.

Before his death here in Togo he called me on his sick bed and told me of a trunk box containing $75m kept in a security company where i amin the city of Sokode. It was because of the wealth he was poisoned by his rivals. I now seek a foreign partner where I will transfer the proceeds for investment as you may advise. I am willing to offer you 20% of the sum as a compensation for your effort/ input and 5% for any expenses that may occour.

Anticipating to hear from you soon.

Thanks and God bless

JACK THOMPSON

From: Bob Servant
To: Jack Thompson
Subject: Greetings

Good morning your Majesty,
I want 30%, and not a penny less,

Your Servant,

Bob Servant

From: Jack Thompson
To: Bob Servant
Subject: I will speak to the bank

Hello Bob,
See these percentages was arranged by the bank and not me. If you insist on getting 30% of the money i have to call the bank.

2   DELETE THIS AT YOUR PERIL

Pls send your

FULL NAME.
CONTACT PHONE NUMBER.
ACCOUNT NUMBER.
COUNTRY/STATE:

I will be expecting those details.thanks.

JACK THOMPSON.

From: Bob Servant
To: Jack Thompson
Subject: Good luck with the bank

Your Majesty,
Let me know what the bank says. Tomorrow's a bank holiday here, I
don't know if you have the same ones? My full name is BOB
GODZILLA SERVANT.

Yours,

Bob

From: Jack Thompson
To: Bob Servant
Subject: Hello

Hello Bob,
I went to my bank. If you are now requesting 30% we have to go
back to the high court to change things. I and my family members
has added some amount upon your money provided you are going to
be serious and trustwordy. We have agreed to give you 25%. Pls i
think that is all we can do.
    We need your telephone number, country, state, city and account
number before we can go further.

Jack Thompson

From: Bob Servant
To: Jack Thompson
Subject: Let's try the court

Good Morning Your Highness,

Please go to the High Court and request the 30%, I think it is a fair figure Jacky-O.

Bob

From: Jack Thompson
To: Bob Servant
Subject: YOUR URGENT RESPONSE NEEDED

Dear Mr Bob,
In order not to waste more time I have agreed the 30% and have notified the court and my family accordingly. Within these few days now, I have developed that confidence in you and believe that you will be of great assistance in perfecting this transaction.
We have to go ahead immediately. Please email me -

1. Your address
2. Private Telephone and Fax Numbers
3. Banking details to enable transfer of the money to you.

I await your immediate response,

Jack Thompson

From: Bob Servant
To: Jack Thompson
Subject: Hold Tight...

Your Highness,
I have been looking at the sums again, and I have decided that I want 40%.

And not a penny less.

Bob

From: Jack Thompson
To: Bob Servant
Subject: URGENT FROM MR JACK THOMPSON

Dear Bob,
Please let us PROCEDE. I am not greedy. I will offer you the 40% instead of delaying the transaction. I want it done, no matter how little it will change my life. Send your details now. Like I told you I

4   DELETE THIS AT YOUR PERIL

need to meet with the security company immediately,

I await an urgent response,

Jack

From: Bob Servant
To: Jack Thompson
Subject: Taxman

Jack,
40% sounds about right. However, I do not want the money in cash, as there is no way I could hide it. The taxman tried to turn me over back in '89 when I was coining it in from the cheeseburger vans, and those bastards always come back.
    Can I have my share in diamonds and gold? I can shift it gradually through pawnshops in Lochee.

Bob

From: Jack Thompson
To: Bob Servant
Subject: URGENT

Hello Bob,
I received your mail and I guess I understand it. As for the diamond and gold, I think I have access to raw gold. You will get your share in some amount of cash and some valuable quantity of gold. Look Bob you are wasting some time in forwarding your details that I need urgently. So now that we have come to an agreement can I have the details now please,

Thanks,

Jack

From: Bob Servant
To: Jack Thompson
Subject: Animals?

Hello Jack,
I'm afraid I just cannot take my share in cash, too dangerous. I could take it in diamonds, gold, or livestock (lions). My neighbour, Frank Theplank, has a private zoo. I just caught up with him in Maciocia's

chip shop where he was waiting on a bag of fifty fritters for his monkeys. I told him a little bit about all this and he is willing to pay $80,000 for every lion I can get him,

Bob

From: Jack Thompson
To: Bob Servant
Subject: URGENT

Hello Bob,
I understand what you mean. You don't want the money in cash. Well I just got in contact with a friend of mine who sells raw gold and I can now pay you through live stock lion heads raw gold...quantity (4). So now you need not worry about the taxman coming again you can always keep them in your friend's private zoo as you said.
    Now I will go and arrange for them while you send me your full details of yourself.

Jack

From: Bob Servant
To: Jack Thompson
Subject: Lions

Hi Jack my friend,
Great to hear from you again. You can get hold of 4 lions? Are they male or female? I will speak to Frank who will undoubtedly be very excited. Where are these lions just now?

Bob

From: Jack Thompson
To: Bob Servant
Subject: URGENT DETAILS PLEASE

Hello Bob,
The gold lions are all male and i have arranged for them. But Bob can't you see you are dragging us backwards i have been asking you for your details for the past days now. Pls reply with the following:

Full Name
Home Address
Phone/Fax Number

DELETE THIS AT YOUR PERIL

Banking Details

I will be expecting the above information.

Thanks.

Jack

From: Bob Servant
To: Jack Thompson
Subject: OK

Jack my friend,
OK, things are now progressing. My full name is, as you know, Bob
Godzilla Servant

68 Harbour View Road,
Broughty Ferry,
Dundee[1]

It's a lovely spot Broughty Ferry, and I stay down near the river.
There's not much traffic which is obviously perfect, as otherwise
the lions would get rattled. Can you please send me a photo of the
lions without delay? I need to see that you definitely have access to
them, before I confirm things with that halfwit Frank.

Your friend,

Bob

From: Jack Thompson
To: Bob Servant
Subject: Details

Hello Bob,
Hope fine. The informations you gave me not complete, you only
gave me your full name and your address. I will need-

Country
State
City
Zip Code
Phone Number

---

1   Bob does indeed live near the River Tay, and in some style, but this address
    does not exist. Just in case anyone was thinking of visiting.

Bank Account

Pls give me the above information then we can proceed. As for the lions I have to take some photographs of them before I scan and send to you, so you have to give me some time. Pls provide me with the remaining information Bob.

Thanks,

Jack

From: Bob Servant
To: Jack Thompson
Subject: Here you go champ

Jack my friend,
What a wonderful morning, hope it's a belter over there in Togo also.

Zip Code - ███████
City - Dundee
Country - Scotland

I'll get the information from the bank later on. The Bank of Scotland in Broughty Ferry closes early on a Wednesday so the staff can go tenpin bowling[2]. Please get the photos of the lions to me as soon as you can, then we can move on. I cannot wait to see those magnificent creatures. Are they currently in captivity, or will you actually be capturing them yourself? By Christ Jack, I wish I were on that hunt with you my friend. Helping you. And holding you.

Yours Faithfully,

Bob G Servant

From: Jack Thompson
To: Bob Servant
Subject: Pictures of the raw lions

Hello Bob,
You didn't include phone number or bank account. I have made arrangement in transporting the 4 gold lions to you. I have put photos below. One costs $299,000 so 4 will cost over $1,196,000 then the rest will be in cash. These gold lions will be bought from a

---

2 The Bank of Scotland in Broughty Ferry does not close early on a Wednesday so the staff can go tenpin bowling.

8   DELETE THIS AT YOUR PERIL

friend of mine's company. So give me your phone number for better communication and bank information,

Thanks,

Jack

From: Bob Servant
To: Jack Thompson
Subject: You have got to be kidding?

Jack,
Sorry about the delay, I was out getting my hair done. There appears to have been a slight misunderstanding my friend, I was expecting four live lions, not gold ones. If I stuck four lion statues in Frank's zoo then he would think I'd lost the fucking plot and would tell everyone that I'd gone mental again like when I first got the cheeseburger van money through and wore that dinosaur poncho for four months. The four photos you sent look great, if a little similar, but I'm afraid that you seem to have got the wrong end of the stick.

Bob

From: Jack Thompson
To: Bob Servant
Subject: URGENT

Hello Bob,
Hope fine. Sorry i misunderstood you, 4 live lions will be much easier for me.

Look Bob, I went to that security company yesterday i was told to get $4000 to process the document for retrieval of the boxes that contains the money. I have raised $2000 so i need you to assist me in the rest of the money. Immediately you send the remaining $2000 I will go to the security company so they can release the funds and I will purchase the lions immediately. I will pay you back the money with percentages.

This is urgent, reply immediately.

Jack

From: Bob Servant
To: Jack Thompson
Subject: No Problem

Jack,
OK, can you send me the photos of the live lions? Where are you getting them? I will speak to the bank tomorrow, but $2,000 sounds fine, how much is that in pounds? The exchange rates in the Dundee *Evening Telegraph* are bollocks, they're done by the same guy that does the horoscopes[3].

Bob

From: Jack Thompson
To: Bob Servant
Subject: HURRY BOB

Hello Bob,
Bob $2000 is £1700. Pls try to send it so I can collect the fund from the security company and as well send the lions to you. These is the lion's picture below. I have made arrangement of transporting it to you. I am buying four male lions from my friends private zoo and he has also arranged for shipment to Scotland.

----

3 This is entirely untrue. Dundee's *Evening Telegraph* newspaper carries a precise reflection of the day's exchange rates.

10 DELETE THIS AT YOUR PERIL

I will prefer you send the money through Western Union transfer, so I can collect the fund and start shipping the lions.

Thanks,

Jack

From: Bob Servant
To: Jack Thompson
Subject: LION PICTURE

Jack,
Greetings my dear, dear friend. Jacky, there seems to have been another misunderstanding. I looked at the website that is listed on the photo of the lion you sent and it belongs a Boston-based author and nature lover.

"I'm Tony Northrup. I live with my wife and cat in Woburn, Massachusetts, which is about 8 miles North-West of Boston", he states quite clearly on his site.

Now Jack, I'm not sure if I can see the connection between

yourself and Tony. Perhaps you sent the wrong photo?

Bob

From: Jack Thompson
To: Bob Servant
Subject: YOU MISUNDERSTAND

Hello Bob,
You are getting this all wrong Bob. I didn't say that was the exact lion, I only gave you a clue on how the lion I will send looks like. If you want to see the exact lion I will send you must give me time to take it and scan it.

So Bob my friend you don't need to worry over this. This is Africa and you well know these animals are sufficient here. My brother even rears a cub that's a baby lioness in his house, so Bob expect the lion's photograph later today. You haven't said anything about the money I asked for? Have you spoken to your bank? I don't think £1,700 should take long to send?

Thanks,

Jack

From: Bob Servant
To: Jack Thompson
Subject: OK, I get it.

Hi Jack,
Thanks so much for putting my mind at rest and letting me know what a lion looks like. I have seen them in the past, in books and suchlike, so already had a fair idea but you have really helped me out there. For example, I had it in my head for some stupid reason that lions wore spectacles.

I look forward to seeing the photo of the actual lions. I just popped my head over the garden wall and had a word with Frank. He was busy cleaning out his Flamengo cage but he did say that he is very, very excited about getting hold of these lions. He has asked me to pass on a few questions -

Are they male or female?
Are they in good physical decision?
Do they talk?

Thank you my friend, and don't worry, I have booked in to see the

DELETE THIS AT YOUR PERIL

bank manager tomorrow morning,

Bob

From: Jack Thompson
To: Bob Servant
Subject: URGENT

Hello Bob,
Hope fine.

Answer to the questions.

1. The lions are all male lions and are very healthy.

2. I don't think I have ever seen a lion that talks.

I don't know if you are also interested in leopards cause my friend
works in the Government Zoo and he could find a leopard for you?
Remember to speak to your bank tomorrow.

Thanks,

Jack

From: Bob Servant
To: Jack Thompson
Subject: Leopards

I have spoken to Frank. He will take two leopards as long as they are
friendly, and one elephant if you can get it? Frank is sure that he
saw a talking lion on the television once. He thinks it was either on
Songs of Praise or Bullseye. He says it reminded him of Jim McLean,
the old Dundee United manager. Are you sure you can't get one?

I am going to the bank in two hours,

Bob

From: Jack Thompson
To: Bob Servant
Subject: URGENT

Hello Bob,

Hope fine. I can get you two leopards. They are both not adults. I will try and see if the elephant will be possible and will see what I can do for the lion. When you are back from bank mail me and tell me when you are sending the money.

Thanks,

Jack.

From: Bob Servant
To: Jack Thompson
Subject: The Full List

Jack,
How are you my friend? Frank just called, he will take the following -

4 lions, 2 leopards, 1 elephant, 1 alligator, 2 parrots, 1 hedgehog.

I said you might be able to get the two leopards and the elephant. How are you looking for the rest? And, of course, the talking lion? Frank has a good few quid. He's worked for me on various bits and bobs and I've always looked after him so I think we should put our necks out on this one and make sure the lions talks.

Bob

From: Jack Thompson
To: Bob Servant
Subject: URGENT

Hello Bob.
From your mail I will only be able to get

4 lions
2 leopards
1 Alligator

The hedgehog, parrots and elephant will take me some time to find but I think I will first send the four lions and two leopards to you before we proceed with the rest. Bob please send the £1,700 now so I can send the 4 lions and 2 leopards to you. I think one of the lions may talk a little.

Thanks,

  **DELETE THIS AT YOUR PERIL**

Jack.

From: Bob Servant
To: Jack Thompson
Subject: Sounds good

Hi Jack,
I will pass on the bad news to Frank on the hedgehog front. I'm not
sure about a lion that only talks a little, I'd like one that isn't so shy
if possible?

Bob

From: Jack Thompson
To: Bob Servant
Subject: THIS IS URGENT

Bob: This is urgent. What is hapening?? I don't sell animals. I only
said I could get some lions to help you. Then you say you need a
leopard and I say ok. Now you are saying the lion has to talk? What
is this madness? Send me the £1700 that we agreed imeediately.

Jack

From: Bob Servant
To: Jack Thompson
Subject: Take it easy Jack

Jack,
What does the lion say when it talks? I am just checking that it
won't get me into any fights.

Your servant,

Bob Servant

From: Jack Thompson
To: Bob Servant
Subject: THIS IS URGENT

BOB LETS GO STRAIGHT TO THE POINT. THE LIONS AND
LEOPARDS ARE HERE WITH ME AT THE BACK OF MY HOUSE THEY
ARE FRIENDLY AND ONE OF THE LION TALKS. BOB SEND ME THE

£1700 SO I CAN COLLECT THAT MONEY AND SHIP THEM TO YOU.

JACK

From: Bob Servant
To: Jack Thompson
Subject: Take it easy Jack

Jack,
Things are coming along nicely. I just need to know, for Frank's benefit more than anything -

What are the names of the lions? (he needs to know what to call them when they are introduced)

What does the lion say when it talks? (Again, who wants a lion that'll get them into scraps?)

The bank is preparing me some forms,

Bob

From: Jack Thompson
To: Bob Servant
Subject: HERE IS THE INFORMATION

Hello Bob,
We have really wasted much time. Anyway, the information you asked for

1. The lion with more hair is Captain

2. The lion with black hair is Zoro

The other two do not have names you can give them names yourself. And as for the lion that talks it's ways of talking are strange. It does not pronounce words well it only makes sounds. Hope you understand now. Bob the security company has given me a day's grace. This is very serious, I don't think you realise what we are about to lose. Let me know when you will send the money and I will give you the info for Western Union.

Jack

16   **DELETE THIS AT YOUR PERIL**

From: Bob Servant
To: Jack Thompson
Subject: All looking good...

Hello Jack,
Sorry about the delay. I was round at Frank's earlier and got stuck up a tree whilst chasing a snake, then fell off and banged my head on a chicken. You know what it's like. Listen Jack, the bank needs to know which account and country the money would be going to?I had extended discussions with Frank at Doc Ferry's bar this evening and he is absolutely delighted with the way things are going. He wants to know a last couple of things -

Can he call the other lions 'FANCY PANTS', and 'BRYAN'?
Do the leopards sing, and are they willing to wear clothes?

All the best babes,

Bob

From: Jack Thompson
To: Bob Servant
Subject: GO TO WESTERN UNION

Hello Bob,
Sorry for what happened to you, hope you didn't get injured. Tell your bank to send the money through Western Union. Money transfer to:

Name: ██████████
Country: ███████
State/City: ██████
Branch: ██████

This is my very good friend name and address that is working in the bank. You will have to set a secret Question and Answer and be sure to send me the answer.
    As for the lions you can call them any name provided you shout when talking to them and always use the same name. And trained leopards like the one I have for you will wear any clothes you buy for them OK. Please send the money today,

Jack

From: Bob Servant
To: Jack Thompson
⟋ **Subject: Nearly back to 100%**

Hello my good friend,
Thanks so much for your kind words. I have nearly fully recovered from the fall and have just been chilling out ever since. I've still got a large bandage on my head however, and am too embarrassed to leave the house as then I'd have to tell people how I got the injury. The boys would love this one. If Tommy Peanuts or Chappy Williams got hold of it I'd not be able to show my face for weeks.

I should be OK tomorrow and will nip up to the bank then. Just a quick question about the leopard, does it look a bit like this?

Good luck my friend,

Bob

- - - - - - - - - - - - - - - - -

  DELETE THIS AT YOUR PERIL

From: Jack Thompson
To: Bob Servant
Subject: URGENT

HELLO BOB,
I HOPE YOU ARE GETTING BETTER. I RECEIVED YOUR MAIL, SINCE
YOU SAID TODAY YOU WILL BE GOING TO THE BANK PLEASE GO
THERE RIGHT AWAY. AS FOR THE LEOPARD THE SKIN ARE ALIKE,
THAT'S THE WAY IT LOOKS LIKE, SO PLEASE TRY AS MUCH AS
YOU CAN TO RECOVER SO YOU CAN BE ABLE TO GO TO THE
BANK. I WILL BE EXPECTING YOUR REPLY SOONEST.

THANKS.

JACK

From: Bob Servant
To: Jack Thompson
Subject: What a Let Down

Jack,
I have some bad news my friend. I have just been to the bank and
the guy there said that I cannot send you any money as I do not
have any in my account. In actual fact, it turns out that I owe them
over eight grand. I tried to explain that I needed to send you this
money for the lions and the leopard but the guy said I was a fucking
lunatic and got the security man to throw me out.
    I'm really sorry Jack, I hope I haven't wasted your time in any
way, I can't see how I could have, but I'm afraid that the deal is off.
Good luck my friend, and good luck with the animals. If they get too
much then you'd probably be OK just releasing them?

Love,

Bob

From: Jack Thompson
To: Bob Servant
Subject: Urgent

Hello Bob,
You see do you really still need lions and leopard? I will help you out
sending it for you free but what you only have to do is to send just
$700 or $500 for shipping it to Scotland.
    If you can go to another bank to send that money to me just

take the money from home and tell them you want to send that money through Western Union money transfer to that name i gave to you earlier on. It is easy. Do it today.

Jack

From: Jack Thompson
To: Bob Servant
Subject: Urgent

Bob?

No Reply

DELETE THIS AT YOUR PERIL

2
Bob and the Postie

From: Jean Kitson
To: Bob Servant
Subject: Employment Format

Sir,

Polysmooth is a UK textile company. We produce and distribute clothing materials worldwide and are looking for people to assist us with a new distribution network.

MAIN REQUIREMENTS

18 years or older, legally capable, responsible, to work 3-4 hours per week, with PC knowledge, e-mail and internet experience (minimal).

And please know that Everything is absolutely legal, that's why You have to fill a contract! If you are interested, please respond with your details. Thanks for your anticipated action.

Very Respectfully,

Mr. President,
Polysmooth International

ENGLAND

Best Regards

Jean Kitson

From: Bob Servant
To: Jean Kitson
Subject: Re: Employment Format

I might be interested Jean. But right now I have some legal problems to take care of.

Your Servant,

Bob Servant

From: Jean Kitson
To: Bob Servant
Subject: Re: Employment Format

  DELETE THIS AT YOUR PERIL

Hope the problem is not that serious but you can share with me if you think i have to know about it.

From: Bob Servant
To: Jean Kitson
Subject: Re: Employment Format

I am in big trouble. Do you know any lawyers?

I have money.

From: Jean Kitson
To: Bob Servant
Subject: Re: Employment Format

Sure, i know some i can introduce you to my lawyer, he is here in the UK, what do you really want? if he can assist you then i'll tell him, hope to hear from you soon

Jean Kitson

From: Bob Servant
To: Jean Kitson
Subject: My shame

Jean,
Great, can you please forward this to the lawyer -

DO NOT JUDGE ME BECAUSE I AM A GOOD MAN.

My name is Bob Servant. You might well have heard of me from the days when I ran the Ellieslea Road to Beach Avenue windowcleaning round. It was Howard Reoch's beat for years but Howie lost it with the OVD and ended up shacking up with a Chinese girl in Lochee and only leaving the flat to get his hair cut.

Anyway, I had to sell the round ten years ago when some little fucker stole my ladders[4]. From there things just turned really bad. I stopped getting work other than from bungalows, and it just wasn't enough to run the van on. So then I was down to bungalows that I

---

4   The story behind the loss of Bob's ladders in 1996 remains unclear. If forced, I would conclude that they were not stolen, but sold as part of the deal through which Bob disposed of his window-cleaning business. However, that should not be seen as evidence in the evaluation of any insurance claim made by Bob at the time.

could reach on foot and there are only really four of them. It got to the stage I was turning up at those four houses a couple of times a week, then nearly every day and they soon rumbled that I was taking the piss and sacked me. So that was me.

Since then I spend my time as a 'man about town'. Sometimes this is a great life, but other times I get quite low. I sit in my house, eating jaffa cakes, drinking cheap wine and building duvet dens in the front room. It's no kind of life, no kind of life at all.

Anyway, I found a way of livening things up, which was to play pranks on my postman. His name is Trevor and he is a complete prick. At first it was basic stuff - I'd grab the letters out his hand and pretend to be a dog, or sit up on the roof and chuck a bucket of water over him.

He complained to the police and they warned me off but that just annoyed me because what did he have to go and tell them for? So I really went to town on him. I built a hide in the garden and took pot-shots at him with an air rifle or chucked a firework at his head. It was really funny. You should have seen his face the time I hit him square on the napper with the Catherine Wheel. I think he might have been crying.

Things came to a head last week. I hid behind a tree and jumped out with a hose but he saw me in time and rushed me. He got his sack over my head but I fought back and managed to get him on the ground. At this point the weasel managed to squirm away but I grabbed him round the top of his trousers and at the same time went for him with the hose.

Unfortunately, he pulled away again and both his trousers and pants came off in my left hand whilst, with my right hand, I accidentally shoved the hosepipe up his bottom. The first I knew was when he let out the most incredible scream, I've never heard anything like it. I threw off the sack and realised what had happened but by that time he was hopping down the path, howling away with the top of the hose still protruding out of his arse. He looked a bit like the Australian kangaroo.

Anyway, to cut a long story short these are the charges that I face as a result of that moment of madness -

ASSAULT
SEXUAL ASSAULT
HARRASSMENT
EXTREME EMBARRASSMENT

I am in court in two weeks - Can you help? What's the best defence? I hope we can work together on this,

Thank you,
Bob

  **DELETE THIS AT YOUR PERIL**

From: Jean Kitson
To: Bob Servant
Subject: Re: My shame

I can help you If you want to help yourself, i was going to give you 7% of the check money we are sending to you, but because of the problem you have I talked to the rest of the company board and they said we would offer you $1000 not $700 and if on the long run you did your job well, you might get rewarded more. What you have to do now is get back to me with all your personal and banking details so we can register you as a worker.

Best regards

Jean Kitson

From: Bob Servant
To: Jean Kitson
Subject: Eh?

Jean,
Thank you for your help but that is no good. I do not need a job, what I need is a lawyer and I need one urgently. I'd use Pop Wood but the guy's legal qualifications are only currently recognised in various Broughty Ferry bars.

Good luck for the future,

Thanks,

Bob

From: Jean Kitson
To: Bob Servant
Subject: I already contacted my attorney

No Bob,
I already contacted my attorney just didn't tell you what he said because I thought you wanted a job. He is willing to come help you at the court so you can be free without charges but he will need you to send him his ticket fee and also pay up front some of the amount to be paid in total after the case is done. Are you also here in the UK, or in another country? Let me know so i can tell the attorney.

Best Regards

Jean Kitson

From: Bob Servant
To: Jean Kitson
Subject: OK

Yes, I am in the UK, up in Scotland. Can you please tell me what the attorney's idea is for my defence? Personally, I think it is very important that I had the sack over my head at the time of the so-called sexual assault. I could not see so how could I have known where the hose was going to go? X-ray specs?

Bob

From: Jean Kitson
To: Bob Servant
Subject: He said he will fill a document

Bob,
OK he said he will fill a document that shows you were not feeling good then and that you didn't do it intentionally, he said that will work. The travelling fee to Scotland isnt much, about £950 plus the upfront money of the case which is all together about £3000. Hope to hear from you soon so I know what to tell the Attorney. Stay safe,

Jean Kitson

From: Bob Servant
To: Jean Kitson
Subject: Chopper?

Jean,
£950 to get to Scotland? Is he coming by fucking helicopter? I think it would be best if you put me in touch with him directly please,

Thank you for your help,

Bob

DELETE THIS AT YOUR PERIL

From: Jean Kitson
To: Bob Servant
Subject: His email

His email is ████████████████████ and his name is Tim
Sanderson. Email him directly,

Regards

Jean Kitson

From: Bob Servant
To: Tim Sanderson
Subject: Hello there

Howdy,
I believe that Jean Kitson has explained my case to you, I am
looking for a lawyer to come and defend me on some trumped up
charges. If you are interested in my case, then please tell me what
you think the best defence would be. If it sounds strong enough, I
will retain you immediately,

All the best,

Bob Servant

From: Tim Sanderson
To: Bob Servant
Subject: Hello there

Hello Mr Servant,
Yes my client Jean has explained things. It would be best for me to
come there so we can put our heads together.You'll have to send
fees then when I come we can talk about your problem. But to start
with I'm a good Lawyer with first Class Upper professional degree
so I believe I can get you out of this mess.

Just one good point I'll make now and the others you will wait till
I come and we can talk better. From the mail Jean passed to me, I'll
say you are at fault but suffered harassment for a long time. So, to
get you out of this mess, a suggestion is putting up a genuine lie
backed up with evidence which the court will accept. I'll tell the
court you had a mental disorder for more than a month (it will
match the time you started this trouble of yours) and will give them
a letter from the psychiatrist hospital.

We therefore plead you didn't know what you were doing so all the harassment, embarrassment, and sexual harassment could be put to an end and the case could be stopped. Well, I think with just this point you are probably already convinced that I am capable to get you out of this?

Hope to hear from you soon, so we could make arrangement on how you are going to send me the money with your details and how to get to you,

Best Regards,

Lawyer T. Sanderson

From: Bob Servant
To: Tim Sanderson
Subject: My defence

Tim,
I like your idea and I think it's just about crazy enough to work. However, I think I may have spotted a slight flaw. Where is the psychiatric hospital you'll get this letter from? It would maybe look a little strange for me to visit London to get my head examined?

By the way, that fucking postie is getting right on my tits again. He knows I can't touch him because of the court case so he's really rubbing my nose in it. When he delivers the mail he shouts stuff through the letterbox like, "Ooh, is this a letter from your boyfriend Bob?" and he sometimes scores out 'Bob' on the letters and writes 'Blob'. I just want to get him again but I have to stop myself because that will just get me in more trouble.

Bob

From: Tim Sanderson
To: Bob Servant
Subject: Just ignore him

Here is my number ██████████ you can call me anytime. But Bob as for him getting on your nerves just ignore him. We will have to go to the nearest hospital to you, the one you are known better, that way it will be easy for us to get the letter.

Stay safe

Lawyer T. Sanderson

DELETE THIS AT YOUR PERIL

From: Bob Servant
To: Tim Sanderson
Subject: Flowers for Jean

Hello Tim,
You're right of course, but it's hard to ignore him sometimes. This morning I heard a tapping on the window and when I opened it he was standing outside urinating all over my front lawn. He was absolutely loving it, spraying everywhere and laughing at me. I don't know how much more I can take before I do something that I regret. I would love to call you but my phone has been cut off because of a Booty Express mix-up. I hope to have it working in the next few days.

I can't go to the hospital here Tim, I'm banned after a misunderstanding back in '94. Dundee United won the Scottish Cup and I read in the paper about how the players had taken the cup to see some sick kids at the hospital. I'd been drinking Snowballs in the Ferry Inn with a couple of traffic wardens (who were on duty at the time!) and so I stupidly decided that I would go and help cheer up the kids.

I made what I thought was an exact origami copy of the Scottish Cup but was really a mess of beer mats and sellotape and went and caught the bus. By the time I got there I was struggling to see but I remember the receptionist telling me that she didn't think my visit would be appropriate. She asked me for my address which I thought was for a Thank You letter but a week later I got a banning order[5]. Not to worry, we can attack them in other ways. Do you agree, for example, we should stress the fact that when the whole hose thing happened, the sack was still over my head? I think this is absolutely vital.

Also, I would really like to send Jean a small gift. She's a classy lady and I don't want to look cheap, but I don't want her to think I'm trying it on. I've got enough to worry about without getting myself a bird! Perhaps she'd like this fun tracksuit?

Bob

---

5   Bob Servant has never received a banning order from any of Dundee's hospitals. I do, however, remember seeing Bob on many occasions in the weeks after United's 1994 cup win struggling with an oversized, tin foil, imitation trophy.

From: Tim Sanderson
To: Bob Servant
Subject: Jean said you shouldn't bother

I talked to Jean she said you shouldn't bother that I should say
thank you and that she only did what she did because you needed
help. When are you ready to send the money and when will I come?

Lawyer T. Sanderson

From: Bob Servant
To: Tim Sanderson
Subject: Good old Jean

Tim,
Typical Jean! What a wonderful woman. No, I want to send her a
present, it's only fair, please give me her address and I'll send some
flowers. Otherwise, I have access to a pedalo that she may be
interested in? The Harbour Police use these to patrol Broughty
Ferry harbour and watch out for Communists[6]. Jean will have to pay
the postage however, which I estimate would be around £1,000.

---

6 Broughty Ferry does not have a Harbour Police service and, even if they
  did, it is unlikely they would use pedalos owing to weather and safety
  concerns.

  **DELETE THIS AT YOUR PERIL**

Anyway, I need to go and set myself up for the postie's arrival, I have a special plan for him this morning,

Bob

From: Tim Sanderson
To: Bob Servant
Subject: Jean said you shouldn't bother

Nevermind about Jean Bob, she did not want anything. I've warned you to leave the postie and not hurt him just ignore him. Look Bob, I won't be having time to reply more of your mail until you pay the fees. This is suffering my other clients. Message me when you want me to come with your address and airport name, and you can mail the money,

Stay safe

Lawyer T. Sanderson

From: Bob Servant
To: Tim Sanderson
Subject: I AM IN TROUBLE

Are you there?

Oh God what have I done?

From: Tim Sanderson
To: Bob Servant
Subject: Yes I am here

Yes Bob. How can I help?

From: Bob Servant
To: Tim Sanderson
Subject: It's got a little spicy

Tim,
It's the postie Tim, the fucking postie. I have him trapped in the cupboard under the stairs. Don't ask me how it happened, all I know is that I got drunk and when I woke up I was lying down in the kitchen. I heard a bit of moaning that I followed and found him. I

have taken a photo for you.

What am I going to do? He says that if I let him go he will not tell anyone but how can I trust him? Would you be able to email me a legal form that he could sign which would say that he couldn't go to the police and tell them?

I know you said £3,000 but if you can get me out of this new scrape I will pay you £5,000 because now I am really worried. If he goes to the police then I think I could be done for kidnapping.I have been looking after him, feeding him jaffa cakes and putting a little radio beside him and he says that he will tell people it was all a misunderstanding, that we were playing a game of sardines and it just got out of hand. But can I trust him?

Please help me Tim, and don't be angry, I know I've been a fool.

Bob

- - - - - - - - - - - - - - - - -

DELETE THIS AT YOUR PERIL

From: Tim Sanderson
To: Bob Servant
Subject: stay calm

I can help with this new situation but only if you pay half of my bills because it is now severe, thats my policy.

From: Bob Servant
To: Tim Sanderson
Subject: Absolutely no problem at all Timbo

Tim,
OK, will do. How much is half the bill? Things are going fine. I've untied Trevor apart from his legs and have been cooking nice meals for him. We had a great pasta dish earlier and I'm going to do a spaghetti Bolognese tonight. He says he's not that bothered about being tied up in the cupboard because it means he doesn't have to go to work and also that he doesn't really like his wife.

Bob

From: Tim Sanderson
To: Bob Servant
Subject: The half bill is

The half bill is £1500. You be careful and don't hurt him because if you do that's going to get you in a big trouble. You have done enough already, message me back with when you can wire the money and I'll send you my info. stay safe.

Tim

From: Bob Servant
To: Tim Sanderson
Subject: half bill

Hi Tim,
£1,500 is no problem. In Dundee's infamous Cheeseburger Wars of 1988-89, I had three vans working double shifts five days a week (I attach a photo of one of the vans in a cracking litle pitch, ready for another bumper day). Those vans were mobbed everywhere they went, it was unbelievable. It sounds funny thinking about it now, but no-one even knew what cheeseburgers were in Dundee before then.

People just went crazy for them[7]. I stuck the boys on £50 a shift and paid fuck all tax. You do the math, Tim

You know, things are great here. I have been untying Trevor completely for one-hour stretches, which we call his 'Cry Freedoms', which makes us both laugh. He can go to the toilet, have a stretch or just potter around the house for a while.

We're getting on well - we both love talking about women and eating jaffa cakes and earlier today he said I was his 'best friend'. I got all embarrassed and angry and tied him up again but, you know, I think he might have meant it. He's not a bad chap and I'm starting to think that maybe he won't tell the police,

Bob Servant

---

7   A 1988 issue of the *Broughty Ferry Gazette* bore the headline, 'This Cheeseburger Madness Must Stop' and included claims from a local councillor that schoolchildren and 'those old enough to know better' were buying their breakfast, lunch and dinner from an 'Armada' of cheeseburger vans. The report quotes 'local cheeseburger magnate Bob Servant' as saying 'I'm giving the people what they want. The councillor will be telling us what time to go to bed next. He's just angry because I wouldn't give him an expenses slip with his burgers'.

DELETE THIS AT YOUR PERIL

From: Tim Sanderson
To: Bob Servant
Subject: Safest way is Western Union

The best and safest way is through Western Union. What you will do is go to the nearest Western Union location to send the £1500. Here is my personal assistant details she will go get the money as soon as you send it cos i'm busy at the office.

Sarah Riley

BIRMINGHAM

That's where she live, she will go get the money. Email me with the necessary details so i can give it to her. Hope to hear from you soon.

Regards

Lawyer T. Sanderson

From: Bob Servant
To: Tim Sanderson
Subject: It's party time

HI TIm,
Are you sure I shouldn't just post the cash? I could tape the money to a bit of card so it doesn't get nicked? Let me know because the £1,500 is ready to go.The postie and I are still going great guns but I think it's important to have a good legal defence just in case.

He's been untied for a couple of days but has not even mentioned going home. We just mess about, playing tig or designing putting courses. I make breakfast, he makes lunch and then the two of us do dinner together. It's a great system, and seems to be working fine.

The only slight problem we have is that I have always watched the evening showing of Neighbours but he is a massive Richard and Judy fan. So far he's settled for watching them until 5.35 and then we switch to Neighbours but I can see he's not happy with it. We have our tea at 5.30 and, yesterday, when I turned over to Neighbours he let some of his scrambled eggs drop onto the carpet and said 'Oh dear, I wonder if one of your Neighbours will help clean that up' in a really sarcastic voice. I did what you told me Tim, and just ignored him. But that's been the only moment that we've looked like falling out.

Tonight we're going to a fancy dress party that the postie's friend is having at his house. I can't wait, he says there's going to be loads of woman there from the sorting office. Apparently, they're going to get blootered and then just go straight to work at five in the morning. They do it once a month apparently, the whole Dundee East Sorting Office, and the next day they just go and put letters in any postbox they fancy because they're still so drunk[8]. So God knows where my mail will end up tomorrow! Or in your case, Timorrow! Ha, ha. Silly.

I'm going to the party as a cowboy and the postie is going as a ghost. Are you going to a party tonight Tim? I bet you are, knowing you. What are you going as?

Bob

From: Tim Sanderson
To: Bob Servant
Subject: Western Union

Send the money to my assistant through Western Union as I said and email me the security details. Hope you are having a great party, i anticipate your response.

Regards

Lawyer T. Sanderson

From: Bob Servant
To: Tim Sanderson
Subject: Good News

Tim,
How are you my friend? Well, well, well, where to begin?! It has been the most mental two days of my life, which is pretty impressive considering I was officially mental for those four months in '89 when I was high on the hog with the cheeseburger van money.

Right, well let's start at the fancy dress party I told you about last time. We got to the door and the postie pressed the bell. Just as they opened the door he whipped his ghost sheet off and he was wearing his best gear - proper denim and a really nice V-neck. So there was him in his Saturday night turn, a couple of birds at the door looking confused, and me dressed as a fucking cowboy.

It wasn't a party at all, he'd arranged a double date with these

---

8   The editor is of no doubt that Dundee East postal staff are of the highest professional integrity and I consider Bob's suggestion to be entirely delusional.

 **DELETE THIS AT YOUR PERIL**

go-ers from his work but thought it would be funny to make old muggins here turn up like Jesse fucking James. The worst bit was he didn't let them in on the joke, when they asked why I was wearing that stuff he told them that it was what I always wore when I went out.

I was so angry I couldn't even bring myself to say anything so I just walked through and we sat and had dinner with me still in the cowboy stuff. The postie was loving it. I tried to make some conversation but anything I said he'd give it 'yee-hah' or 'sorry we don't have any cow pie' which isn't even a cowboy joke, it was Desperate Dan that ate cow pie.

I was pretty annoyed and, I suppose, a little bit hurt and threw a bit of a tantrum. I shouted at the postie that he had let me down, that I had trusted him, and he'd made me look stupid. I went right off on one and I could see the girls were scared but I just kept going. At the end there was this horrible silence and then the postie started whistling the theme tune to Rawhide.

And you know what Tim? I laughed. That's right, I laughed. I laughed and I laughed and so did the postie and so did the girls and we just all started hugging each other. And then we were kissing and then one thing led to another Tim and, well, I won't say any more on that.

Tim, it was sensational. It's been a long time since I got properly involved with a bird and I have to say that I was worried old Bobby might not have much in the locker but by Christ I went to town on that bit of skirt. You should have seen me Tim, I was like a man possessed, I felt like a bloody kid up the back of the pictures.

Well, since then things have really gone very well indeed. The postie and I have decided that we are going to live together and spend our time chasing women like a couple of wild cards - throwing on the denim, downing some liveners, then heading into town and seeing what happens. Ach, we're probably just two old dreamers without half a brain between us Tim! But, my God, we'll give it a go.

So really it's all good news. The postie has promised me that he will drop the charges. Thanks for your help Tim and please thank Jean also. I know you'll both be happy for me, being the kind of people you are.

All the very best for the future,

Bob Servant

From: Tim Sanderson
To: Bob Servant
Subject: Western Union

I am glad things have gone well, please send £500 for the advice I gave you. Send it through Western Union to the details I provided.

From: Bob Servant
To: Tim Sanderson
Subject: Hands off the party fund!

Sorry, Tim. We have to watch our pennies as the postie has quit his job so he and I can chase skirt professionally. I'd be happy to act as a reference for any similar cases you find yourself involved with if that's any use?

Cheers,

Bob

No Reply

DELETE THIS AT YOUR PERIL

3

Alexandra, Bob and Champion

From: Alexandra
To: Bob Servant
Subject: Hello!

Hello, my new friend! My name is Alexandra, 25 years old. I live in Russia and want to get acquainted with man from other country. Be not surprised to my letter. I have learned your address in agency of international acquaintances. I do not know, like you my photo or not? At once I want to say I do not search the relation for games. I want to find the husband! I shall expect answer with impatience!

Best wishes, Alexandra

P.S. Please, send to me your photo.

From: Bob Servant
To: Alexandra
Subject: By Christ You Could Take Someone's Eyes Out With Them

Alexandra,
How are you? What a fantastic photo. My God, what a pair of bazookas. How is life over there in Russia?

Your Servant,

Bob Servant

  DELETE THIS AT YOUR PERIL

From: Alexandra
To: Bob Servant
Subject: Hello!

Dear Bob!
I am very glad that you have answered my letter! It is a pity, that you have not sent me the photo. It is a problem for you? I live in city Vladivostok. Probably, you think me beautiful and think, that at me it is a lot of admirers. Yes, I shall not begin to deny it. But I do not like the Russian men, their attitude to women. I want to love and be loved. Unfortunately, I have not found it in the country. I am gentle women but I am a tiger when I am in love!

Alexandra

From: Bob Servant
To: Alexandra
Subject: YOU LIKE THE TIGER? I LIKE THE LION!

Alex,
A tiger eh? I can certainly sympathise with anyone who has a love of large cats, being an enormous lion fan. A lion is tough, it's bloody tough, but it doesn't bully people and has a great sense of humour.
    A funny thing happened to me today in Woolworth's Alex. I was walking past Geronimo McLardy the security guard, when he whispered to me
    "I don't need no brothers to do my busting, I just need the booty to do some cusping".
    Do you understand, very roughly, what he was saying?

Bob

From: Alexandra
To: Bob Servant
Subject: OK

I do not understand fully about what your friend speaks.It seems to me, that you are frivolous a man. You would like to play only? Where is your photo? What can you offer me to make me love you?

From: Bob Servant
To: Alexandra
Subject: Chill out

Alexandra,
I apologise, let me give you a little more info. I'm Bob Servant and I am a semi-retired window cleaner from Broughty Ferry. I gave up my round when gypsies nicked my ladders, and I suppose that looking back that was my greatest mistake. But, as you are no doubt aware, I had already done very, very well from the cheeseburger game. I have attached a photo of myself from a recent fishing trip[9]. What do you think? About me, not the fish!!

Bobby Boy xx

From: Alexandra
To: Bob Servant
Subject: A question

The Fish is simply magnificent!:) And it is possible an immodest question? How old are you?

From: Bob Servant
To: Alexandra
Subject: IT WAS A GREAT FISH AND VERY TASTY TOO!

Alexandra,
Thank you for your kind words. That is one of the largest fish I have

---

9 This man is not Bob Servant. I have no idea who he is, but the fish looks like a mirror carp.

DELETE THIS AT YOUR PERIL

ever caught. It nearly ripped my bloody arms out. Do you fish much? I used to nip up to the Monikie reservoir with Frank Theplank. We had some good days. He brought the sandwiches and I brought the beers. But you know what Frank's like, not the brightest, and one time we got there and I whipped out the beers then he whipped out his Tesco bag and inside were his nephew's football boots. I was fucking raging and we never went again. I am 62 years old, but I am as fit as a fiddle.

Bob

From: Alexandra
To: Bob Servant
Subject: Age

It is very a pity, Rob, but it seems that we are not created for one another...To me 23 years, you - 62 years. What prospects of our relations? Let's look at things really. What can you offer me? Your humour?

From: Bob Servant
To: Alexandra
Subject: It's your call monkey face but I do like you!

Alexandra,
One thing before we continue. I see you chose to call me Rob there. I can only hope that this was a one-off as that is one thing that I simply cannot allow. I remember Tommy Peanuts telling me that Bob Wilson beat a jockey half to death live on Grandstand in the early 1980s after the jockey called him Rob[10] and I have to admit that it makes me just as mad. It's Bob or nothing Alexandra, and that's that.
You are a frank woman and that is one of the things that I love about you, along with your looks and your admirable interest in big cats. I am looking for a woman, no doubt about it. My success has left me a man of leisure here in Broughty Ferry. I buy supermarket Finest meals, drink premium pints, and often go for the one-man banquet from the Peking Garden even though I will never, ever, finish it.

I have a hell of a lot of cash at my disposal Alexandra. But don't tell the taxman! I have a wonderful house, though it could certainly do with a woman's touch. And I have a fantastic voice, very smoky

---

10 There is no record of the former international goalkeeper turned television presenter Bob Wilson ever having physically attacked a jockey, either on or off air.

but also surprisingly gentle. It's your call Alexandra. What I will say is that I think you are beautiful and I am excited about our relationship. I also want children. And believe me - there is lead in this bloody pencil.

Bob x

From: Alexandra
To: Bob Servant
Subject: Hello!

Dear Bob, never Rob!
It was very pleasant to receive from you these answers! You very interesting!

At leisure I like to look cinema. I like film " Forrest Gump " where a leading role has played Tom Hanks. It is very good film, where many various philosophical ideas and ideas. I also very much like to dance. I could learn to dance you!

If you want to write to me the letter, my full post address: ██████████████, Vladivostok, Russian Federation. I think that a meeting is necessary for us! We already can name each other good friends. I am right? I like your sense of humour. I tell my good friends about you,

Alex

From: Bob Servant
To: Alexandra
Subject: LOOSE LIPS COST LIVES

Hello love. It is nice to hear from you but there is something very important I should tell you. Please, Alex, you cannot tell anyone about me. I work for a man called Don Cabbage. He's a bit like Don Corleone, except he's from Broughty Ferry. And his name genuinely is Don. But he's still a gangster. Some of the stuff we get up to is pretty dodgy – selling photocopied disabled parking tickets, homemade jazz mags, and Viagra ice cream (though we've not made any of that yet).

Bob

From: Alexandra
To: Bob Servant
Subject: A secret?

  DELETE THIS AT YOUR PERIL

Bob, OK, I understand, that you have secrets in work. I promise
to nobody speak about you. But, why it is a secret? You like me
more and more. Can we meet New Year together? We shall make a
mad act? I can arrive to you. If the idea has liked - answer quickly
and we shall discuss details. Your little monkey Alex :)

From: Bob Servant
To: Alexandra
Subject: New Year

Alex,
Merry Christmas[11]! You would like to come here, to Broughty Ferry,
for New Year? My God, that would be fantastic. I'm not sure what
my plans are. Stewpot's Bar is throwing in a finger buffet and a
magician and Chappy Williams is having a fancy dress party so we're
well covered. I'll have to tidy the house up. Alex, what is your stance
on jazz mags? I have probably about 2,000 of the fuckers but I
would be willing to bin them if you're going to get on your high
horse about the whole thing,

Bob x

From: Alexandra
To: Bob Servant
Subject: Yes, I do!

I want to meet New Year together with you. I have the passport and
good friends in a travel company, which can issue the visa. I
understand that you are on illegal position and can take cares that
your name will not be mentioned.
    I can take holiday for 2 months but there is a banal problem.
Money. I did not plan trip now. That is I openly speak, that I have no
financial opportunity. If you have an opportunity to help me with
money then our meeting will be a reality and we can meet New Year
together!

Your Alex

---

11 This email was indeed sent by Bob on Christmas Day, an impressive
    dedication to his hobby, and this entire exchange was very intense, with up
    to a dozen emails a day between Christmas Day and New Year. When I
    mentioned this to Bob he pointed out that he refuses to watch television at
    that time of year because of the special festive scheduling (which he
    describes as 'an insult to his intelligence') and so had a fair amount of time
    on his hands.

From: Bob Servant
To: Alexandra
Subject: OPPORTUNITY AT STEWPOT'S

Alex,

I love the Christmas period, it really shakes things up. I must say, I am delighted by you wanting to come over here for New Year. I think it is a daring decision and I admire that about you Alex. You are a strong, exciting woman who knows when to stand up for herself. You are a fighter Alex, like Rocky Balboa or Martin Luther King. You believe in freedom (your own). I'll tell you what, this old world is a hell of a lot better for having you around.

Alex, I've been thinking of what we will do when you come to live here. I am a man of means, there is absolutely no doubt about that, but I worry you'll be bored with nothing to do other than hang about with old Bob. I was thinking that perhaps you could take a part-time job? Stewpot's Bar has a note up for a lunch waitress. It would only be 12pm-3pm Monday-Saturday with Wednesday off and every other Tuesday being a 2pm finish because of the OAP domino league.

What do you think? I was in there today and mentioned to Terry Darcus the landlord that I had a Russian woman coming over to see me at New Year who might fancy the job but, you know what Terry's like, he just started laughing and walked off.

I've been working on your uniform and I've come up trumps. Nothing too revealing, I'm putting my foot down on that. The last thing I need is you flashing your bits at the boys in Stewpot's. So you can forget that right now or the whole bloody thing's off as far as I'm concerned. I was thinking a t-shirt with 'Bob's Bird' written on the front and 'Stop Looking' on the back?

Bob

From: Alexandra
To: Bob Servant
Subject: Job is not problem

My Darling Bob!

I agree to work some time as the waitress. It would be amusing:) It is valid, it will help me to earn money and in training to English, you are right.

You to me are very interesting and want to see you now! But to issue the visa for such short time, additional financial assets will be necessary. It is necessary for me of 1000 euros that the visa was ready this week. I want to pay for air tickets itself. But money for the visa are necessary already tomorrow!

46   DELETE THIS AT YOUR PERIL

Yours Alex.

From: Bob Servant
To: Alexandra
Subject: TERRY'S BEING A BASTARD

Alex,
I popped in to see Terry this morning and he said that you have to fill in an application from. I said I'd vouch for you and he said the last person I vouched for was Frank Theplank, who he employed as a kitchen porter but had to sack after a day when Frank kept sending out meals with carrots carved into nobs. So you have to fill in the form. I tried to talk him round but you know what Terry's like. Send me back the answers as soon as possible and I'll take them in.

WHAT IS YOUR FULL NAME?
AGE?
WHY DO YOU WANT TO WORK IN STEWPOT'S?
WHAT DO YOU THINK YOUR BEST SKILLS ARE?
DO YOU PROMISE NOT TO CARVE CARROTS INTO NOBS?
ARE YOU HONEST?

All the best,

Bob

From: Alexandra
To: Bob Servant
Subject: My Answers for Terry

Dear Bob!
I have just received the letter and I answer your questions.

WHAT IS YOUR FULL NAME?

My full name: the Name: Alexandra the Surname: Dadashov

AGE?

My age: 25 years and 5 months:)

WHY DO YOU WANT TO WORK IN STEWPOT'S?

I want to work during my trip to you to not be to you a burden and consequently, that I like to work, communicate with people. I do not like to idle.

WHAT DO YOU THINK YOUR BEST SKILLS ARE?

I specialize on Russian cuisine more. But I can prepare the Italian and Mexican cuisine also.

DO YOU PROMISE NOT TO CARVE CARROTS INTO NOBS?

:)))) Certainly. But suddenly it clients will want? For me desire of the client - the law:)))

ARE YOU HONEST?

For all time of the life I tried to communicate with people fairly and to deceive nobody. For me the bitter truth is always better than sweet lie. Yes, I am fair with you 100%.
So, I hope, that have answered all your questions. Now answer you and it is maximum fast. When you can send me 1000 euros the visa?

Alex

From: Bob Servant
To: Alexandra
Subject: Special Russian Riddle Needed

Alex,
I have some news. I spoke to Terry just there but it was absolutely rammed in Stewpot's because the Dundee United game was on. I tried to speak to him at half time but I couldn't get near him because he does free sausage rolls and he got mobbed the minute he came out the kitchen. I was in there with Tommy Peanuts and he said it was like Beatlemania.
Things calmed down a bit in the second half though so I managed to have a quick word with him. I told him that you were very interested in the job and with living with me in Broughty Ferry and him and Tommy started laughing, I'm not sure what about. I gave him your application form and he said it looked promising and that he'd look forward to seeing you.
On the way home I bumped into Chappy Williams coming out the bookies. I said that we wanted to come to his New Year party and he told me that it's now-

CHAPPY WILLIAM'S SPECIAL NEW YEAR TALENT SHOW

DELETE THIS AT YOUR PERIL

He said that we can only come if we agree to do a special talent act that lasts at least two minutes. Any ideas? One thought I had was that we could go to the party as

THE MYSTERIOUS CURTAIN PEOPLE.

We would wear my old curtains over our heads and just cut tiny, tiny slits into them so we can see where we are going on the way to Chappy's. We would cut through Forthill because if we walked through the Ferry dressed as curtains we'd have all sorts of jokers having a pop.

At Chappy's we would wear the curtains and only talk in riddles when people ask who we are. We could talk in foreign accents. For you this is easy. I'll probably speak like a Frenchman.

If someone asks me who I am then I'll say -

Oooh, I really don't know
But I do like corn on the cob
If you were to say a name that sounds like this
Then you will have done a good job

What could you say? Do you have a good Russian riddle? It is a fun game, and I need to show Chappy that we have it all worked out. Then we can plan your visa,

Bobby x

From: Alexandra
To: Bob Servant
Subject: a riddle?

Dear Bob!
As I could understand, you require a riddle... That is I should represent the woman whom of other country, but I should not speak, what I from Russia? I have understood?

From: Bob Servant
To: Alexandra
Subject: WE'RE NOT GOING TO GET THE GOLDEN TICKET WITH THAT RUBBISH

Alex,
Come on, we'll have to do better than that. If you stood there in a curtain mumbling about representing women from other country then people would think you were insane.

It is very, very important that we manage to get an invite to Chappy's do. Everyone who is anyone in Broughty Ferry is going to be there and it is a wonderful opportunity to introduce you to local society.

You need a riddle of four lines that says you are from Russia but only through clues.

Bob

From: Alexandra
To: Bob Servant
Subject: Dear Bob!

Dear Bob!
I at last have understood. Ok, but it not last variant:) So...

1. I from the country which knows all world but which nobody understands...
2. I from the country which language hardly is easier, than Chinese:)
3. I from the country, where the most beautiful girls in the world:)
4. I from the country where do not mark Christmas on December, 25:))

You will accept?

Yours Alex

From: Bob Servant
To: Alexandra
Subject: BAD NEWS BUT ALL IS NOT LOST

Alex,
How are you my darling? OK, first the bad news. I finally caught up with Chappy Williams last night at Khan's kebab shop and talked him through your curtains plan.

I told him the riddles and he didn't like the idea at all. He said that they were no good and also pointed out that my old curtains were my Dinosaur ones and everyone would recognise them because I wore them as a poncho for four months when the cheeseburger money came through.

Chappy said we weren't offering enough of an actual talent to take part in the event. He reckons, and I guess he's right, that sticking curtains on your head and speaking in riddles isn't a recognisable talent. I know it seems harsh but Chappy has only got

  **DELETE THIS AT YOUR PERIL**

a one-bedroom flat and there has been a lot of interest. I was at Berkeley's Butchers earlier and four of them are going as Bananarama, and I know for a fact that Big Dom Maciocia has put together a Jackson Five from his chip shop.

So, I'm sorry Alex, but the party's off. I still want you to come though. I am confident that you will win the role at Stewpot's and I'm desperate to see you. I want someone who can join me for walks along Broughty Ferry beach, or at the couples only nights at the bowling club, or as medical support and motivator during my monthly crack at the Dawson Park monkey bars record. You, Alex, are that woman.

But first, we need to get a few things straight.

1. Jazz Mags

I have approximately 2,000 jazz mags hidden all over the house. I don't read them that much, but Don Cabbage makes me keep them in case he gets turned over by the police. I give some away, and guys like Frank Theplank and Tommy Peanuts are always borrowing them, but most drawers and cupboards in the house have at least one jazz mag in them. As does the fridge and the freezer. And the oven. And all of my jackets, some of which are lined with them.

Do you want me to clean up the jazz mags into one, easily monitored pile? You could maybe limit me to one mag a week, or maybe I could only be allowed to read them if you were out with the girls for a glass of wine, or in hospital having been run over. What do you think?

2. Apron

I have a novelty apron I wear when I am making dinner, and some other times too. It makes it look as if I have a women's body and am wearing a brassiere and women's pants. Is this acceptable?

3. Cartoon

A few months ago, Archie Campbell won the bowling club's monthly Saucy Cartoon Competition[12] with something he got off the Internet. It was a typical stunt by Archie, all flash and showing off, so I told him it was rubbish and not as funny as Garfield in the Dundee Courier. But the thing was, Alex, that the cartoon is actually very funny indeed. When Archie wasn't looking, I popped it in my pocket and stuck it up on the kitchen wall when I got home.

Basically it's a job interview and the man says 'so you can't keep

---

12 No bowling club in the Broughty Ferry area admits to holding such an event.

a secret, well you've still got the job' to this woman. It's funny because keeping secrets is important but, here's the thing, the woman's bazookas are hanging out! So he gives her the job anyway!

It cracks me up and having it in the kitchen is a good way of starting the day with a smile.

What do you think? Do you see this as a bit of fun or are you going to get all angry and say it's not fair on the woman even though she's just a cartoon woman? Maybe you'd rather have a photo of babies up in the kitchen, or a calendar so you can mark up when you're going to the barbers?

Let me know what you think about these things please Alex, so I can start getting things ready for you here.

Bob x

From: Alexandra
To: Bob Servant
Subject: Money for visa needed now

My darling Bob!
I shall answer your questions. But if I shall not pay the money today then I cannot receive the visa! You understand?

1. It is not necessary for you "to clean up the jazz mags into one, easily monitored pile". As I have understood, jazz mags is a part of your life which you very much value. What for to pretend to someone to anothers? So leave like you have usually.

2. Mmm. This threat looks sexually:) To me is not a problem to carry it:)

3. To me too it is very interesting Cartoon. I find it amusing and I hope, that when we shall be together we shall cheerfully look at it together:)

I hope, that have answered all your questions. Now I shall tell you cost has increased to 1300 euro because additional expenses for renewal of documents are required. You should inform me when you can send me this sum. And tell me what airport I should come to? Do you like photo I send to show my love?

Alex

  **DELETE THIS AT YOUR PERIL**

From: Bob Servant
To: Alexandra
Subject: WHAT A CLEVER PHOTO!

Hello Alex,
What a clever photo! At first I thought it was just you blowing old
Bob a kiss and then I looked at the computer screen and there was
old Bob himself! Great stuff. A nice idea, well executed. I think it's
probably best that you fly to Edinburgh airport. I can get Geronimo
McLardy to drive me there to pick you up. He'll do it for jazz mags.
Oh, what a wonderful day that will be!

When the bank opens I am going to ask for the money for your
visa. To hell with the cost!

Love,

Bob

From: Alexandra
To: Bob Servant
Subject: Visa

Hello Bob,
Once again the information on how you should send the money -

1. Name of the addressee: Alexandra
2. Surname of the addressee: Dadashov
3. City and country of the addressee: Vladivostok, Russia

I hope, that you can make it in the nearest hour because our banks work only up to 3 PM.

Alex

From: Bob Servant
To: Alexandra
Subject: THE HEAT IS ON

Alex,
I have had a terrible day. This morning, Don Cabbage turned up and said I owed him money so he was going to live in my house for a while. I have had to cook for him and pour him drinks and all he does is laugh and ruffle my hair really hard. Don has one thing he does called 'The Angry Dove'. He twists his hands together and kind of waggles them like wings and says 'Oh, oh, the dove's getting angry' and then attacks you with the dove. Well, not the dove, with his hands. He punches you in the face, basically, with the dove's wings. Well, they're not the dove's wings. They're his fists.

What should I do Alex? I am scared and frightened and it seems like my whole world is collapsing onto my knees and shins. Sometimes I wish I had never got involved with Don Cabbage and a life of crime for the last couple of years. Yes, it's given me a lot, but it has also taken away a lot and now Don Cabbage is living here, in my house.

Please write back soon. I am too scared to check the email when he is around but whenever he naps I will sneak over and check.

Bob

 **DELETE THIS AT YOUR PERIL**

From: Alexandra
To: Bob Servant
Subject: We have no time for this!

My darling Bob!
I was bothered with this. I lose time, money and patience. The question on my reception of the visa is solved tomorrow. If you will not send me money our meeting will be unreal because the embassy will not give me the visa. Really for you it is difficult to understand it? If for you money not a problem why you cannot make it now or tomorrow? To me has bothered to waste time, money and my reputation. You still have time and we can be together.

Alex

From: Bob Servant
To: Alexandra
Subject: I AM TRYING MY BEST FOR GOD'S SAKE

Alex,
I am trying my darling but it is very hard for me with Don Cabbage being in the house all the time. He is a very scary man. I have some money here, around £5,000 but I do not want him to know I have this money do you see? Once he leaves I can go and send it to you from the Post Office.
  Earlier, Don Cabbage went to the bathroom and I went to look in his room. He has some bad things in there Alex, including an axe and some really big potatoes that I think he uses as missiles. I am very scared Alex, what should I do? As soon as he leaves I can send you the £5,000. Please write back and please understand, I love you but my life is in danger from Don Cabbage,

Bob xx

From: Alexandra
To: Bob Servant
Subject: We have not much time

Darling Bob
I know you are scared but I am already tired to wait for hours with you of a meeting. You must be quick,

Alex

DELETE THIS AT YOUR PERIL   55

From: Bob Servant
To: Alexandra
Subject: WONDERFUL NEWS

Alex,
I have some fantastic news. Don Cabbage has left! He said that
someone in Lochee owed him £15 for some jazz mags and he went
off to get him. He says that if I keep my nose clean then he'll leave
me alone for while. Thank God for that!

So we're back on track! I have the money here to make our
dreams come true! How quickly could you be here? I have a surprise
for you. I have bought something that I think you will like. I will give
you a clue. You need to feed it. Can you guess?

Bob

From: Alexandra
To: Bob Servant
Subject: Hello

Bob!
I did not want to lose good relations with my friends in a travel
company. I have already informed you, how you can help me. You
can have a way to any branch Western Union. I have made all for
this purpose. If you will not help me, I shall be compelled to give in
parts 1300 euro to my friends within several months. I think now
that you play with me?

Yours Alex

From: Bob Servant
To: Alexandra
Subject: OH COME ON ALEX, DON'T BE LIKE THAT!

Alex,
What kind of weirdo would spend all this time emailing you if they
were not serious? I have the money to send to the Western Union in
Vladivostok but what is the point in sending you money when you
are suggesting that I am some sort of joker? I have even bought you
a present, it was supposed to be surprise, but maybe if you see it
then you will understand that I am serious.

Yours in hope,

Bob x

  **DELETE THIS AT YOUR PERIL**

From: Alexandra
To: Bob Servant
Subject: I am sorry

My dear Bob!
I am sorry for behaviour. I am very tired... I very much want to be
with you. You should understand, that for me it is very difficult to
accept again the man. But you have very much liked me, I do not
hide it. And now I shall be very glad, if our meeting with you will
take place. I wait for concrete actions. I am very much intrigued
with a gift which you have prepared me?

Alex

From: Bob Servant
To: Alexandra
Subject: READY?

Alex,
Ok, apology accepted. Are you ready to see your present?

Bob x

From: Alexandra
To: Bob Servant
Subject: Yes!

Yes, certainly, I am ready to see my present:))

From: Bob Servant
To: Alexandra
Subject: HERE WE GO! HE'S CALLED CHAMPION!

From: Alexandra
To: Bob Servant
Subject: I like it

My dear Bob!
Your gift has very much liked me, very originally. Still anybody similar in life did not give anything to me. Now about our affairs. I very much hope, that today you will make that for a long time promised me...to Western Union! I expect your answer...

Alex

From: Bob Servant
To: Alexandra
Subject: NOT LONG NOW!

DELETE THIS AT YOUR PERIL

Alex,
I am so excited that you like your present. I was going to Carnoustie on the bus the other day when I spotted Champion in a field. 'Aye, aye', I thought, 'What's going on over there then?' So I got off the bus and went to have a good look at the blighter.

Now, Alex, just about every household in Carnoustie owns at least one ostrich[13] but for some reason the farmer hadn't shifted Champion. The next thing you know we'd shaken hands on me to take Champion off his hands for £150, eight jazz mags and the spice rack I won in the bowling club Christmas raffle.

So tomorrow I'm going to get up, have a quick bite to eat at Stewpot's Bar and a couple of liveners, then nip up to Carnoustie on the bus and pick up Champion. Then I'll come back here, tie him up in the garden and race round to the Post Office to send the cash. Are you looking forward to seeing me and Champion?

Also, do you have any idea what I should feed Champion? Would he eat chips?

Bob x

From: Alexandra
To: Bob Servant
Subject: Let us resolve this today now

Send the money as the most important part of your travels tomorrow. Certainly, I very much wait happily for our meeting. It will be better, if to my arrival the Champion will be little bit hungry then I could feed him:) Chips? He loves chips? I never saw ostriches earlier, it is very interesting to me:))

Now I wait from you for the information on a remittance that I could continue the preparation to be with you and Champion.

Alex

From: Bob Servant
To: Alexandra
Subject: A rollercoaster of a day

Alex,
An unforgettable day. I went along to Stewpot's first thing and told all the boys I was off to pick up an ostrich for my Russian girlfriend and they were giving it, 'Oh aye, your Russian girlfriend Bob, is that

----

13 Although no exact measure can be given (you do not need a licence to purchase an ostrich, which I found surprising) a quick check with local RSPCA officials suggests that this claim is untrue.

the one that's going to work here?' and I was saying 'Yeah, that's her, Alexandra' and they all started laughing.

So it was a good atmosphere and then they started saying that Russian men can drink a bottle of vodka straight and if I couldn't do that then you would leave me. Well, I wasn't going to risk that so I told Terry to line me up his best bottle and a couple of cheese sandwiches.

Now, I'm a drinker Alex, I've never hidden that from you but I have two Achilles heels. The first is strong women and the second is vodka. They just don't agree with me and after an hour or so it all got a bit blurry. Then suddenly I was alert again but someone had stolen one of my sandwiches so I went round the pub asking who had my sandwich but people just kept laughing.

Then Terry told me to look in the mirror behind the bar and I saw that the sandwich was stuck to my forehead. I must have fallen asleep onto it or something. So I took the sandwich off and left Stewpot's in the huff and went to catch the bus to Carnoustie.

It was quite hard because my legs weren't working properly but I got on the bus OK and then gave everyone a laugh with some animal jokes and a bit of a sing.

I got off the bus fine though I did fall into a hedge. When I found Champion he was in great form. I didn't have a lead so I took off my jumper and stuck it over his head and used a sleeve to lead him out back to the bus stop. I was feeding him some pork scratchings when the farmer appeared and went absolutely berserk.

He was saying stuff like, 'what the fuck do you think you're playing at?' 'get that fucking jumper off it's head' and 'you're a fucking basket case and I'm going to call the police'.

I kept my dignity and ignored him and he went off to get the police, but then the bus came. The driver must have been texting his mate or something because he actually stopped and I had Champion halfway on before he even noticed. He got scared and said there was no way I could bring an ostrich on the bus and I said to just charge him half fare but then the other people on the bus started getting involved (even though it was none of their business) and were all screaming and stuff.

Of course, that set Champion off who went totally bananas, lashing out with his feet and pecking away. He lifted a woman's bunnet clean off and caught a man with a moustache an absolute beauty on the side of the head. "That's one peck on the cheek you didn't ask for!" I said, to lighten the mood but the guy didn't get it, he just rolled about holding his head and swearing at me.

Then the police turned up and so I went to have a wee chat with them but tripped and went into another hedge. I don't remember much after that, just the police standing about and then Champion being led off by the farmer. I shouted 'See you later Champion, you can keep the jumper' but he didn't reply.

The policemen brought me home and said I might get done for

DELETE THIS AT YOUR PERIL

cruelty and fined, so I might need that money that I was going to use for your visa. I'm sorry about Champion but, to be honest, I don't think it's safe to have a family pet that could go off the handle like that.

And, anyway, all is not lost! I went to Doc Ferry's bar to have a think about things and bumped into Chappy Williams. I told him what happened and he said he had something in the car I could have. He went off and came back with a bloody dog! I couldn't believe it. Chappy had really red cheeks and was out of breath but seemed to find everything very funny. I asked what it was called and he said 'Bob' so I said, 'But that's my name' and he said that I should call it 'Bob The Dog' so I don't get confused.

It was hard walking home with Bob, he didn't seem to be listening to anything I said but we're back now and I think he's sleeping. I'm sorry about the money thing but I hope that you can maybe come over here using your own money and I'll pay for the groceries. And the food for Bob. Bob the Dog I mean, not me.

Love,

Bob. Not Bob the Dog! He wouldn't be able to write!

From: Alexandra
To: Bob Servant
Subject: Re: a rollercoaster of a day

Fuck you! To me has bothered to read your delirium

No Reply

 DELETE THIS AT YOUR PERIL

4

Uncle Bob's African Adventure

From: Joseph Udeze
To: Bob Servant
Subject: Are you interested?

Dear Good Friend,
I am Joseph Udeze, solicitor at law. I am the personal Attorney To Mr Christian Clark, a national of your country, who lived in Nigeria. In May 2000, my client was killed in a car accident in Kano. The bank where he had an account of $9.5m has issued me a notice to provide the beneficiary or have the account confiscated within 20 days.

Since I have been unsuccessful in locating the relatives, I now seek your consent to present you as the beneficiary of the $9.5m. If you agree, we can discuss your percentage. Please i will like you to send to me your full name and address, private telephone and fax number for easy communication.

Best regards,

Barr. Joseph Udeze (Esq.)

From: Bob Servant
To: Joseph Udeze
Subject: Good morning

Joseph,
I cannot help you with the Clarky stuff, but if you can prove that you live in Africa then I have a business proposal for you,

Your Servant,

Bob Servant

From: Joseph Udeze
To: Bob Servant
Subject: FURTHER DETAILS

Dear Bob,
Yes! I live in Africa and as such would be ready for your proposal.

Thanks,

Joseph

DELETE THIS AT YOUR PERIL

From: Bob Servant
To: Joseph Udeze
Subject: Now we're talking...

Joseph,
Listen my new pal, I have an idea that I would like to run past you. I think, and hope, that it will blow your socks off. I have a small cafe here in Broughty Ferry. We mostly work off the taxi drivers and posties, you know the drill - sausages (link and square), bacon rolls, meths. You'd be amazed at the meths we shift Joseph. Around half the posties that work out of Dundee East Sorting Office are on the meths day and night. I heard from Tommy Peanuts that a couple of them actually get paid in meths[14].

Anyway, to cut a long story short, I want to give the cafe a total overhaul. I'm happy to close the place down for two weeks and really go to town on it.

What I'm thinking is this -

UNCLE BOB'S AFRICAN ADVENTURE

I would fill the place with plants and trees and make it really dark. When people came in they would literally have to trek to the counter, using a machete to get through the vines and avoid being attacked by the lions. These would be large paper mache lion heads that I would wear, popping up from behind the foliage and roaring in their ears.

Let me know if you think you could help,

Yours,

Bob

From: Joseph Udeze
To: Bob Servant
Subject: I am waiting...

Dear Bob,
Nice talks...I shall be willing to render assistance if you can give to me further details. You have made a nice catch! How can I help with this enterprise?

---

14 This pair of claims is, quite obviously, complete nonsense. Not only does the Royal Mail's Dundee East Sorting Office have no record of methylated spirits addiction, the theory that any of the postmen there would be paid using methylated spirits is entirely inaccurate and, indeed, ludicrous.

DELETE THIS AT YOUR PERIL

Thanks,

Joseph.

From: Bob Servant
To: Joseph Udeze
Subject: What I need

Joseph,
That is great news. What I need is this - an African team that can come up with sizzling African dishes that the cafe can cook. And, fuck me Joseph, I need it now. What do you think? I would need full recipes and would be willing to pay $500 for each one. Right now, I urgently need two genuine African recipes for which I will pay $1,000 by Western Union.

I need -

The name of the dish
The ingredients needed
Instructions for cooking

I am incredibly excited about this. I am going to close the cafe next week and start the work on it.

Yours,

Bob Servant

From: Joseph Udeze
To: Bob Servant
Subject: OK

Dear Bob,
I have just read your mail, and I am sure that gradually I understand what you are talking about. All is well and like I assured you before now, I can do that for you. Africa as continent has a lot of dishes, but if I am to get correct answers to your request, then I have to concentrate on Nigerian dishes which I am very familiar with. I shall be responding further in that regards. Thanks for consulting me!

Joseph.

  **DELETE THIS AT YOUR PERIL**

From: Bob Servant
To: Joseph Udeze
Subject: An announcement

Joseph,
I hereby appoint you -

HEAD OF MENU CONSULTATION at UNCLE BOB'S AFRICAN
ADVENTURE.

That's right, you've got it. I have given you an opportunity Joseph,
do not let me down,

Uncle Bob

From: Joseph Udeze
To: Bob Servant
Subject: My true position on the matter

Dear Bob,
I have read your mail this morning and it is my sincere wish to help
you. Like I stated, I am a lawyer by profession and as such would
want to handle any transaction that I am having with anybody
legally so that we don't end up misunderstanding ourselves. Before
we can commence actions so please forward your full personal
details.
    Meanwhile I have consulted a specialist in Food Technology and
that is to give to you the best of satisfaction in your demand. An
investment has to be made and that is why I need to be assured
that you would not let me down because as a professional in that
field, I am required to pay to him consultation fees. Let me know
your considerations over this..
    Thanks and I am wishing you a successful endeavour.

Joseph U.

From: Bob Servant
To: Joseph Udeze
Subject: Sounds good

Joseph,
Good to hear from you my friend. Things are coming along really
well here. Old Joan, who works behind the counter, has taken it upon
herself to start learning Swahili, which is a lovely touch. I think she
was worried that I was going to sack her and get in someone

younger and more exotic when we reopen and it's great to see the staff on their toes like this.

I have a very, very good feeling about UNCLE BOB'S AFRICAN ADVENTURE. I think we are going to wipe the floor with the competition, in particular ARCHIE'S PIT STOP. Archie and I used to be friends until one night a few years ago. We were at the bowling club getting pissed up and I stupidly told Archie how well my cafe was doing.

He'd just got £20,000 redundancy from the Michelin and the next thing you know the bastard has opened up ARCHIE'S PIT STOP one hundred yards down the road from the cafe. We've never spoken since and I hope that I drive him to the wall. By Christ, he'll near enough shit himself when he sees UNCLE BOB'S AFRICAN ADVENTURE. I can't wait.

That is great news about the food technician. He sounds just the calibre of person that we need to get on board. Please welcome him to the team from me.

Also, here's the other info you need -

I'm single/available

Cafe address -

Uncle Bob's Wonderful Cafe
71 The High Street
████████████
Dundee,
Scotland
UK

Look forward to hearing from you my friend. How long until the first recipe? Have some fun with it Joseph - surprise me and tease me, feel free to sauce it up, but not too spicy please.

Uncle Bob

From: Joseph Udeze
To: Bob Servant
Subject: Have a look at the attached files

Dear Bob,
I have read your mail and also saw your information. I am still wanting to know your age. Thanks for all the information which has given me more confidence in what we are about doing. As I promised you in my early morning mail, I have attached here

68   DELETE THIS AT YOUR PERIL

scanned copies of my own photographs for your perusal[15].

Thanks,

Joseph.

From: Bob Servant
To: Joseph Udeze
Subject: Sensational

Joseph,
Thank you so much for sending me these photos. They are simply
sensational. In the first one you look extremely smart and have
really turned yourself out nicely. In the second, you have been
captured brilliantly relaxing with your family. The photos, if you like,
show the two sides of Joseph Udeze, am I correct?
  You look quite like Sir Trevor MacDonald, who used to read the news
over here and play for Newcastle United[16]. Is he a relation of yours?

---

15 Mr Udeze also provided a family photo which has been removed for legal
   reasons.
16 I can only speculate that this is a weak joke aimed at Newcastle United's
   1970s centre forward Malcolm 'Supermac' Macdonald. The newscaster and
   television presenter Sir Trevor MacDonald has, quite evidently, never
   played professional football.

Thank you,

Bob

PS I am 62 years old.

From: Joseph Udeze
To: Bob Servant
Subject: Thanks for your words

Dear Bob,
All is well, thanks for your words. I shall be getting to you tomorrow
further information as soon as I have spoken with the food
specialist. Just relax your mind because I am working things out in a
way that favors everybody.

    I have just viewed a picture on the web of Sir Trevor MacDonald
and I am not related. People can resemble each other and that is
exactly what you have spotted. I don't think I have any relation over
there in Scotland.

Have a nice time.

Yours truly,

Joseph U.

From: Bob Servant
To: Joseph Udeze
Subject: Frank

Joseph,
Hello my friend, good to hear from you and don't worry about the
Sir Trevor MacDonald thing, it doesn't affect your employment.
Joseph, I really need to get these recipes in as my chef Frank
Theplank has to start practising very soon so that he can cook them
by the time the cafe opens.

    Frank is not the sharpest knife in the box and he is already
bloody furious with the African theme, so I am keen to get him
working on them asap. I will get Frank to email you directly. Please
send the recipes straight to him to save time and then email me to
arrange payment,

Many thanks,

Uncle Bob

  **DELETE THIS AT YOUR PERIL**

From: Frank Theplank
To: Joseph Udeze
Subject: RECIPES

HULLO
I AM THE CHEF AT BOB SERVANT'S CAFE AND HE TOLD ME TO
EMAIL YOU AND ASK FOR THE AFRICAN RECIPES WHICH YOU ARE
SENDING US FOR THIS STUPID NEW AFRICAN CAFE HE IS MAKING

FRANK THEPLANK

From: Joseph Udeze
To: Bob Servant, Frank Theplank
Subject: From the chef

Forwarded Message -

From: Christian Bala
To: Joseph Udeze
Subject: African Menu

ATTN: MR. BOB SERVANT /FRANK THEPLANK,
I AM CHRISTIAN BALA (CHEF). HAVING RECEIVED INSTRUCTIONS
FROM MR. JOSEPH UDEZE, I WILL OUTLINE SOME OF THE
POPULAR AFRICAN DISHES. I SHALL ALSO BE WILLING TO BRIEF
YOU FURTHER ON HOW THEY ARE PREPARED TO GET THE BEST
OF TASTE AS SOON AS WE HAVE AGREED TERMS.

BELOW ARE SOME FOR THE MOMENT:-

1) ABACHA (AFRICAN SALAD)

INGREDIENTS: - CASSAVA (SHREDED), UGBA (OIL BEAN), PALM
OIL, CRAYFISH, GARDEN EGG, HERRING FISH, COW HIDE (KPOMO),
UKAZI LEAF, SALT/PEPPER.

2) YAM PORRIDGE.

INGREDIENTS: - YAM, PALM OIL, CRAY FISH OR SHRIMPS, PEPPER,
GREEN LEAF OR PUMPKIN VEGETABLE, WATER LEAF, SMOKED
FISH, SALT.

3) UGBA (OIL BEAN)

INGREDIENTS: - OIL BEAN (SHREDED), STOCKFISH, PALM OIL,
CRAYFISH (GRINDED), CRABS, PEPPER, POTASH, SALT.

4) ISI EWU (GOAT HEAD)

INGREDIENTS: - GOAT HEAD, PALM OIL (RED), CENT LEAF (NCHANWU), POTASH, GREEN PEPPER, SALT, OIL BEAN (UGBA)

5) AFANG SOUP.

INGREDIENTS: - WATER LEAF, OKAZI LEAF, BEEF/FISH, PERIWINKLE, SNAILS, CRABS, PALM OIL, PEPPER, SALT.

I SHALL BE WAITING FOR YOUR COMMENTS.

CHRISTIAN BALA

From: Bob Servant
To: Joseph Udeze, Christian Bala, Frank Theplank
Subject: MENU

Joseph/Michael,
Good news, the cafe is coming on brilliantly and UNCLE BOB'S AFRICAN ADVENTURE is really starting to take shape. I am trying to get hold of a camel and have put an advert for one in the window at Toshy's Hardware. Once Frank has got your dishes nailed we're going to be in business. I have chosen 3 dishes below, send the full instructions to Frank Theplank,

Bob

YAM PORRIDGE

ISI EWU

AFANG SOUP

From: Christian Bala
To: Bob Servant, Joseph Udeze, Frank Theplank
Subject: More on African Menu

ATTN: MR. BOB SERVANT /FRANK THEPLANK,
EVERYTHING WILL BE AS YOU DESIRE. I AM WORKING OUT MODALITIES WITH JOSEPH TO FIGURE OUT THE MOST EXCELLENT WAYS TO DELIVER THE INSTRUCTIONS SO THAT YOU DO NOT MAKE MISTAKES.
    I WANT YOU TO JUST COUNT ON ME FOR A SUCCESSFUL "UNCLE BOB'S AFRICAN ADVENTURE" THAT WILL CAUSE

  DELETE THIS AT YOUR PERIL

TRAFFIC-JAM (HOLDUP OR GO-SLOW) IN SCOTLAND. WE ARE ALSO WISHING TO KNOW HOW MUCH YOU INTEND TO PAY US FOR THE SERVICES WE HAVE DESIRED TO RENDER?

THANKS,

CHRISTIAN BALA

From: Frank Theplank
To: Bob Servant, Joseph Udeze, Christian Bala
Subject: Yam

IS YAM JUST AFRICAN FOR HAM?

From: Bob Servant
To: Frank Theplank, Joseph Udeze, Christian Bala
Subject: Appointments

Hello everyone,
Firstly, some official appointments. I think this is the best structure for you guys over there (or 'The Recipe Boys', as I like to call you when talking to Old Joan), and us cats here in Broughty Ferry. So here's the lowdown -

Joseph Udeze - Menu Consultant
Christian Bala - Food Technician
Frank Theplank – Head Chef
Bob Servant – Owner and Inspiration/Father Figure
Old Joan – Cashier

NB Joseph Udeze and Christian Bala also can be collectively referred to as 'The Recipe Boys'. (as long as they're OK with that)
  What do you think? With this team we will not only stop traffic, as you say, but blast Archie's Pit Stop into oblivion. Send the recipes to Frank Theplank today. He will check them over. If everything is fine then I will pay you $500 each recipe and then order some more immediately. So get your thinking caps on Recipe Boys!
  The cafe is now closed and undergoing refurbishment. I am going down to Homebase this afternoon to buy the foliage for the jungle theme and I'm going to pop into Remnant Kings and see if they have much in the way of animal skins.

Uncle Bob

PS Frank, yam is not ham. I will explain more this afternoon.

From: Christian Bala
To: Bob Servant, Frank Theplank
Subject: AFRICAN MENU (The Yam Potage)

MENU NO: (1) THE YAM POTAGE,

INGREDIENTS: --- YAM, PALM OIL, CRAY FISH OR SHRIMPS,
PEPPER, ONION, CENT LEAF, GREEN LEAF OR PUMPKIN LEAF,
WATER LEAF, SMOKED FISH, SALT ETC.

HOW TO PREPARE YAM POTAGE: --- PEEL YAM - CUT INTO CUBES,
WASH AND PUT IN POT. ADD WATER THAT COVERS THE YAM. ADD
PALM OIL AND BOIL THEN PLACE ON BURNER (STOVE, GAS
COOKER E.T.C). BOIL FOR 5 MINUTES THEN INTRODUCE SPICES
SUCH AS CHOPPED ONIONS, CENT LEAF (NCHANWU) TO GIVE
YAM POTAGE FLAVOR, GRINDED PEPPER AND CRAY FISH OR
SHRIMPS. THEN ADD SMOKED FISH AND OTHER VEGETABLES
AND BOIL UNTIL YAM IS READY FOR EATING.

HOW TO SERVE YAM POTAGE: -- NORMALLY SERVED HOT IN TWO
DIFFERENT BOWLS - BOILED YAM IN ONE PLATE WITH BROTH
(SOUP) IN OTHER. A SET OF CUTLERIES (KNIFE, SPOON AND
FORK) IS USED TO EAT YAM POTAGE.

ENJOY YOUR MEAL! THIS IS JUST THE TIP OF THE ICEBERG! I
SHALL BE WAITING FOR YOUR COMMENTS,

CHRISTIAN BALA (CHEF).

From: Bob Servant
To: Christian Bala, Joseph Udeze
Subject: The Yam Potage

Christian,
Thank you very much for this recipe. Frank is not working today as
he trapped his foot in a drain on the way home last night and is
unable to walk. With anyone else I would find this suspicious but,
with Frank, I believe it. The guy is a complete fool. However, he is a
good chef and I can't wait to see how he does with these recipes.

Can you please send us the other two recipes today? Then I can
get Frank to cook all three tomorrow when he comes in. Once he's
done that, and assuming that they are as delicious as they sound,
then I will order more and pay you for the three.

I attach a photo of Frank[17]. It's important you know what the

---

17 This is not Frank The Plank, and no negative conclusions should be drawn
    about this man. If anything, he looks like a fine man.

Scottish gang looks like over there at Recipe HQ. Also, I'm going to start hunting about for a lion's head. Should I get a male or female? I know the easy answer is male but sometimes I think female lions are more scary because you wouldn't expect it from them. I don't want one that's too scary though as it would be disastrous if I were to give someone a heart attack. Maybe I'll just wear a normal tracksuit with the lion's head so they realise it is not a real lion,

Bob

From: Christian Bala
To: Bob Servant
Subject: Payment

Dear Bob,
You will be fine with male or female lion head as people will be terrified of both. Your café will be a big success. We are ever willing to render every services that you desired, but would not do so unprofessionally.

We have released the information on how to prepare Yam Potage as a sample of what we are capable of doing. We are also willing to release the other two menus but it is our wish to demand for at least an advance payment to proceed with the assignment which we are very willing to accomplish. Your good understanding would be highly appreciated.

Thanks,

Christian Bala

From: Bob Servant
To: Christian Bala, Joseph Udeze
Subject: Bad news

Gentlemen,

I have bad news. Archie, that idiot, has been coming round the last couple of days and winding up Frank and myself. I take him with a pinch of salt but unfortunately Frank gets very angry with the teasing. Archie keeps tricking Frank by making him say words that he says are African but really they are just bad words spelt backwards. You know, the usual - DRATSAB, and so on.

Anyway, yesterday he really went to town on Frank when I was up at the bank sorting out some change. I came back in and Frank was wearing a lion outfit that had been superglued up the back. Archie had told him it would help him cook African food and then glued him into it. Poor Frank was absolutely roasting, still trying to make that Yam Potage but it was very hard for him as he could hardly see out the eyeholes. Also, a group of local children saw him through the window and came in and started throwing things at him.

When I arrived I saw one hit him on the head and another jab him in the bottom with a rolling pin. Actually, the guy who did that was in his late 40s. I told him I could understand the kids messing about but it was a bit much him getting involved. He apologised and said he had been attracted in from the street by the kids laughing and found himself getting sucked into the whole thing.

I managed to clear everyone out but Frank was absolutely livid. I got the suit off and he just sat there, rocking on a chair, saying 'Pit stop, Pit stop' over and over. I didn't know what to say. I told him to take the rest of the day off and he just got up, smiled and said, 'Goodbye Bob. I'll take care of it'. The funny thing is that he looked so peaceful when he left.

I got on with work (I've been trying to draw palm trees on the wall but they just look like big seagulls) and then a couple of hours later I heard sirens. I ran down the street just in time to see Frank dancing in the flames of what used to be ARCHIE'S PIT STOP, wearing the lion outfit.

  **DELETE THIS AT YOUR PERIL**

There was nothing I could do and the police were there immediately and carted him off. As he passed me he shouted, "Say goodbye to the Recipe Boys" before they dragged him off. There was something strange about him though, and it was only when I looked closer that I noticed the llon outfit had some form of liquid all over it.

Frank was covered, you've guessed it, in Yam Potage.

Of course, there's no way I can continue with the business now. Frank was a wonderful chef and, in many ways, was also my rock. I am going to sell up and go back into window cleaning. Thank you so much for all your work, it's just lucky that it wasn't wasted,

All the very best for the future,

Bob Servant

**From: Christian Bala
To: Bob Servant**

YOU ARE A STUPID MAN

No Reply

5

The Sea Could Not Take Him, No Woman Could Tame Him

From: Colin Jackson
To: Bob Servant
Subject: Job Offer

Good Day,
My name is Mr Colin Jackson an artist in the United Kingdom. I have been selling my art works for the last 3 years to galleries and private collectors all around the world but am always facing serious difficulties as people are always offering to pay with financial instruments that I am not familiar with.

I undergo so much difficulty in converting them to cash and am currently in search of a representative who I am willing to pay 15% each transaction. You would receive payments, convert them to cash, deduct 15% and send the remaining funds to me. If you have read and understood my offer, please indicate your willingness to work for me.

Best Regards

Colin Jackson

From: Bob Servant
To: Colin Jackson
Subject: I would love to see your work?

Colin,
Thank you for getting in touch and for thinking of old Bobby boy for this unique proposal. You sound like a fine fellow and well done on sticking with your art. So many creative folk give up at the first hurdle and it is really heartening that you have swum against the tide. Could you possibly email me some examples of your work? I am currently looking to redecorate and maybe they could be just the ticket!

Your Servant,

Bob Servant

From: Colin Jackson
To: Bob Servant
Subject: Here you go Bob

Hello Bob,
Thanks for getting back to me, i really appreciate you taking your time to reply to my job offer and also being interested in working

  DELETE THIS AT YOUR PERIL

with me as a business partner. I have attached a picture of my artwork as you asked, hope you will love it and it becomes my ticket lol!

Actually why i need you is as a cashier where you take out your percentage as agreed from every payment. Since you the first person to respond to my offer then I will consider you as my first choice of cashier which am going to give a trial? The information i will require from you will be

Your Full Name
Full Address
Contact Phone

Next we will talk about banking details. Hope everything is being understood here, waiting to hear from you.

Colin Jackson

- - - - - - - - - - - - - - - - -

From: Bob Servant
To: Colin Jackson
Subject: You have an exceptional talent

Colin,
Thank you so much for sending that example, which is a stunning piece. I've always been a plum fan and, I must say, I had a hunch that you would be too. I love art Colin, and I always have, but it's hard being an art lover here in Broughty Ferry. Frank Theplank once told me that his favourite artist is Rolf Harris and I know for a fact that he wasn't joking. I don't have much time for Harris since he shot that dog on the telly[18].

---

18 Bob is presumably referring, erroneously, to a 1994 edition of *Animal Hospital*, presented by Rolf Harris, where a German Shepherd called Floss was put down on medical grounds. Far from being involved in the dog's death, Harris was visibly upset by the incident.

I would love to buy some of your art Colin. There you go, I've said it. I don't have much in the house and I think that sticking a few paintings up would really brighten up the joint as well as being a big hit with any skirt that comes round.

Do you have any paintings of ships? I live right beside the river Tay and I often sit in the garden, especially in the summer, drinking cider and watch the boats messing about out there. I think it would be great to have a few boats on the walls in the house. There's another reason as well for me wanting a boat painting, to be honest, but I'm a little embarrassed to say.

Hope you're having a nice weekend. It's raining cats and dogs here. Good weather for ducks!

Bob

From: Colin Jackson
To: Bob Servant
Subject: Thank You

Thanks Bob,
It's a pleasure hearing from you, I am truly flattered. I have not many paintings of ships but I do have one that is below[19]. Do you like it? Let me know what you think and also if you are still going to work with me as a cashier or a customer? It is a cashier I need but I will not turn down a customer! lol sounds funny Bob.

Thanks again for your mail looking for your reply.

Colin

From: Bob Servant
To: Colin Jackson
Subject: A Proposition

Colin,
That is absolutely enchanting - a sleepy harbour scene on a summer's morning, if I may be so bold! It is so life-like Colin, I feel like stripping naked and diving through my computer screen into the water, though I'm so drunk I'd probably miss and end up wedged in the bin. That would be just my bloody luck.

---

19 At this point Mr Jackson provided a wonderful photo of a harbour scene but the image was badly corrupted. When I informed Bob of this he responded that he had some photos at home that were 'a lot more corrupt than that'. This was an observation that Bob found so amusing I momentarily thought he may choke to death on his sandwich.

DELETE THIS AT YOUR PERIL

I would prefer a slightly different painting. As I touched on before, there is something else I should tell you. You see, Colin, I used to be in the Merchant Navy. It was during my wilderness years before I hit the glory days of the cheeseburger vans. That much is true but in actual fact I never set foot on a boat.

I was dismissed after two weeks training for a misunderstanding. On our last lesson a female instructor was talking us through some First Aid. With it being the last day, spirits were running high and one thing led to another and I put my hand up the instructor's skirt. It was just a bit of harmless fun Colin (I only waved it about up there to get some laughs, no funny business), and this was the late 1970s so you'd think it would have all blown over but the fuckers said it was out of order and kicked me out[20].

Anyway, when I talk to the boys in the bars of Broughty Ferry I have occasionally exaggerated my Merchant Navy career. I've told them all sorts - that I captained my own ship called 'Bob's Beauty', that I had a Chinese wife and that I once knocked out a shark off the coast of Jamaica with a head butt.

What I would love is a painting where there is a man in quite a big boat but you can't see his face? Then I could say that it is a painting of me in 'Bob's Beauty' from the late 1970s. Maybe you could paint some flares on the man. What do you think? I have a fair bit of money stashed away for situations like this, which arise a lot more than you'd expect.

Bob Servant

From: Colin Jackson
To: Bob Servant
Subject: I could do this

Ok Bob,
 Really a funny story bob, what you are asking for is not impossible i can do it for you, with your name printed on it like you said 'Bob's Beauty' but its going to cost you quite a lot of money for such a thing.

It is not a problem for me but you have to pay part of the money in advance to assure me that you will pick it up so my effort won't be wasted. so if you wish then send me the following -

Your picture that you will like to see on the painting

---

20 I think, for Bob's sake, I should confirm that this incident did not occur. He did apply for the Merchant Navy in 1975 but never heard back from them. He believes this was due to the fact that he included a nude photo with his application to demonstrate his physical prowess.

The color combination that you wish

The advance of $1000 then the balance of $1500 when your painting gets to you
    I will be updating you on how the work progresses. The money should be sent through Western Union. I will be waiting for your mail,

Colin

From: Bob Servant
To: Colin Jackson
Subject: Anything kicking about your studio?

Colin,
Great to hear from you. I'd love to get this painting on the go but I worry that if you paint the thing from scratch then it will take bloody ages. I'm having a 'Pernod and Push-ups Party' in a fortnight and I'd really like the painting for that. Do you have a painting of a man on a boat that we can just pretend is me? Maybe it's in the distance so people would not know? If so, then I could just buy that,

Bob

From: Colin Jackson
To: Bob Servant
Subject: I have one

Hello Bob,
Really do not have the exact painting you are looking for but something close to that, picture below. Let me know what you think. I am happy to sell it but it is a little expensive[21].

Thanks

From: Bob Servant
To: Colin Jackson
Subject: Bob Looking out to sea

---

21 Here Mr Jackson kindly sent a photo of a contented-looking gentleman looking out with binoculars at a sunset from a ship's bridge. An action, I should say, that I have always been led to believe could lead to instant blindness. Anyway, the photo contains certain identifiable aspects and I have therefore reluctantly removed it.

84   DELETE THIS AT YOUR PERIL

Colin,

That is perfect. I think we could call it 'Bob Looking Out To Sea' and say it shows me looking out from the bridge of Bob's Beauty, looking for icebergs perhaps? What do you think? Does that sound believable to you?

One thing I noticed was that, in the silhouette of my image I am wearing a floppy hat. I don't think that this is what a captain would wear and attach a photo of a more appropriate hat for the final image.

Your friend,

Bob

From: Colin Jackson
To: Bob Servant
Subject: You must decide

Hey Bob,

It will be a lot of work for me to edit the hat on the already made painting with the one you have sent me, is almost a new job so Bob but I will do. Let me know so we can save time instead of this stress. If you wanted a new painting it would have been almost ready by now! So make up your mind and let me know.

Thanks

Colin

From: Bob Servant
To: Colin Jackson

Subject: Painting

Colin,

Maybe I should go for the existing painting. I could tell people that the reason I was wearing the floppy hat was because it was taken during my break? What do you think? Would you believe that? And, more importantly, would you believe that if you were a woman Colin?

I am desperate to fix something up on the skirt front because Tommy Peanuts recently got together with Daphne Silverstone, the barmaid at Stewpot's Bar. Daphne, I must admit, is a real diamond. She's not as young as she was (she's 68) but my God she still has them hanging over the bar down at Stewpot's. I'm sometimes one of the hangers myself! She does all sorts of shit, leaning over for the peanuts like she doesn't know why we order them, or making saucy comments that send us wild.

Whenever someone orders an apple juice she'll give it – 'Oooh, I feel quite fruity myself', and do that thing where you pretend your eyeballs are rolling backwards into your head. Or if a punter asks if they do sandwiches she'll say, 'Ooooh, are you asking if you can nibble on my buns?' and do the old double-point at her boobs[22] while everyone cheers and bangs their glasses on the bar.

It's all basic, knockabout stuff but with Daphne it just doesn't seem tacky, do you know what I mean? Anyway, Tommy has somehow squired himself up with Daphne and he is ABSOLUTELY BLOODY LOVING IT. Christ, he's walking about the Ferry like he's John Wayne and he keeps pretending to have a bad back just so he can wink and make some rude comment about how he got it.

So the pressure's on old Bob here to come up with something. And I think this painting could be my way in.

Bob

From: Colin Jackson
To: Bob Servant
Subject: Yes I would believe this for sure

Hey Bob,

I think that's exactly what you should tell them, that the picture was taken during a break. Anybody will believe that. Women as well, and this painting will be a big help on you find your own Daphne. Are we now agreed? I can do a special deal but you will have to pay in advance.

Colin

---

22 Stewpot's Bar in Broughty Ferry has never employed a barmaid that behaves in such a manner. 'More's the pity,' said Stewpot when I asked him.

  **DELETE THIS AT YOUR PERIL**

From: Bob Servant
To: Colin Jackson
Subject: YES YOU'RE RIGHT COLIN

Hi Colin,
I think you're right. No-one can see my face or anything like that so as far as they're concerned there's no reason why the figure in the painting shouldn't be me. Even captains have to take breaks sometimes. Also, I was thinking I could buy a hat like the one in the painting and start wearing it about so if anyone at the party said it wasn't me I could say 'Of course it is, you must have seen me wearing this hat?' and pull it out and they'd have no choice but to agree.

Colin, I would love to see a photo of you at work on a painting or in a studio, is this possible? I'm not being nosey! I just love artists and it would be fantastic to see you at work?

Many thanks,

Bobby

From: Colin Jackson
To: Bob Servant
Subject: Myself in studio

Hello Bob,
How are you doing? I am OK just been a little busy with work. You should know i am a busy man...lol.

My pictures at work attached below[23], then i would really like to make a fresh painting of you in Bob's Beauty? You must finally make up your mind once and for all and tell me what you think i am not always able to check my mail. Looking for your mail. ASAP.

Thanks

Colin

---

23 At this point Mr Jackson supplied several photos of an artist working in a studio. The images have been removed for legal reasons. They're perfectly pleasant shots, they're just very unlikely to feature Mr Jackson.

From: Bob Servant
To: Colin Jackson
Subject: Painting Final Order!

Colin,
Great to hear from you and thank you so much for those pictures. I love seeing you working, you look as if you are totally lost in the moment, adrift in the world of art.

I have decided! I want a large painting of the image you have shown me, with 'Bob' (wink wink!) looking out to sea. I would like it framed in a gold frame, or one that looks gold (wink wink!) and underneath I would like the inscription -

'Captain Bob Servant bravely looks out from the bridge of Bob's Beauty. Valentines Day, 1978, somewhere in the Indian Ocean.'

and then, underneath that, the quotation.

'The Sea Could Not Take Him, No Woman Could Tame Him, No Mountain Too Tall, No River Too Deep, Deep Like His Heart. Bob Servant, Simply The Best. Rocking All Over The World'.

Does that all sound OK? I would like the painting to be done in a gloss finish and to measure 2m long and around 1.5m high as that would look magic above my second sofa. I am very excited by this Colin, very excited indeed.

Bob

PS I had a bit of a debate with Chappy Williams at the Eagle Inn last night Colin. As an artist, do you think in words or pictures? I said I thought you would think in pictures but Chappy said that was a load of shite?

From: Colin Jackson
To: Bob Servant
Subject: OK

Hello Bob,
Thanks again. All the same artist speak both in words and pictures. Remember we have our home, friends, family and social life to live so we speak only in pictures when we are at work Bob! Then about your painting i will do the art work and all the words you want me to print on it sounds OK because it makes you look like a brave captain or rather a hero, lol.

I looking forward to get your mail ASAP and it very important that you send your advance through Western Union so I can get started on Bob's Beauty!

  DELETE THIS AT YOUR PERIL

Then the job will be ready within 12 days.

Have a super day,

Colin

From: Bob Servant
To: Colin Jackson
Subject: You have missed the point entirely

Hi Colin,
I did not mean you would speak in pictures, I was asking if you THINK in pictures. If I was to walk up to you in the street and whisper 'mmmm, hello Colin, you look good', then would you think in words 'BOB THINKS I LOOK GOOD' or would you see YOURSELF as a PICTURE, looking the best that you can? That is what I am interested in. Is it different for you, as an artist?

Bob

From: Colin Jackson
To: Bob Servant
Subject: I now understand Bob

Ok Bob,
I got your mail its alright, I will commence with the Job as soon as you send the advance.
   Yes Bob we do think in pictures, I have spent more than 90% of my adulthood in studios painting and thinking of what my customers will appreciate making it as real as possible. When I go shopping with my wife i often stare at things that are around me, imagining them in pictures and dreaming of making paintings of everything I see.
   Well hope u are having a nice day. Let me know when you have sent the money Bob.

Colin

From: Bob Servant
To: Colin Jackson
Subject: YOU'RE GOING TO BE IN THE PAPER!

Colin,
I have interesting news! First of all, I have the money ordered and

will have it tomorrow. The second is that I was just in the Royal Arch looking for skirt and bumped into Chappy Williams again. Apparently, he has just landed the big one - Broughty Ferry correspondent for the Evening Telegraph[24]. Christ only knows how he got it, he reckons he took a grand off the deputy editor at a poker lock-in at Stewpot's bar and they settled for him getting the gig[25].

Anyway, I spoke to him about the fact you were doing this painting for me and he was very, very excited. He put down his cocktail (sex on the beach), turned to me and said, 'Fuck me Bob this could be big'. We chatted about it all some more, and he says that he wants to interview you for the paper! I have had problems with both the local press and my general reputation in the last few years. Or, if I'm being honest, decades. This is an opportunity for me to really bounce back. I told him that you are a busy man so he is only going to send you a few questions. Thanks so much, I will send you the article when it comes out.

Please make me sound like a fun guy when you send Chappy your answers. And, Colin, REMEMBER, two things -

He thinks I was a real captain of Bob's Beauty! Make sure you say that.

Please say that I am very handsome if he asks. That will help me with the skirt and Christ knows I need all the help I can get.

Thank you my friend,

Bob

PS 90% of your life in the studio? That seems a little high?

From: Colin Jackson
To: Bob Servant
Subject: Interview

Hello Captain Bob,
Thanks for your mail and interest in me, but I want to know will the interview be through mail or something? Secondly I will do just like you said {captain in the Bob's Beauty} so you have nothing to worry about because we are in this together.

Then about the money how did you send it? You should send it through Western Union or Moneygram as it will be available for pick-up instantly. You need to send it now, it is very important as we

---

24 No Chappy Williams has ever been employed by the Evening Telegraph, nor has the paper ever had a 'Broughty Ferry correspondent'.

25 The suggestion that the deputy editor of the Evening Telegraph would hand out an editorial posting to clear a gambling debt is outrageous and has no basis whatsoever in fact.

  **DELETE THIS AT YOUR PERIL**

must get this thing started. Let me know when you have done this and Bob's Beauty will kick off.

Have a wonderful day.

Colin

From: Chappy Williams
To: Colin Jackson
Subject: Interview

HELLO COLIN I AM CHAPPY, A FRIEND OF BOB SERVANT AND A TOP NEWSPAPER REPORTER. I HAVE SOME QUESTIONS FOR YOU FOR AN EXCLUSIVE INTERVIEW. PLEASE SEND ME THE ANSWERS AS SOON AS YOU CAN. THANK YOU, CHAPPY.

How long have you been an artist and what was it that made you start?

Bob said that you think in pictures, can you please explain?

How did you meet Bob?

You are doing a painting of Bob in a boat, is it true that he was a captain in the merchant navy? (I have my doubts)

Do you think he is handsome?

What is your favourite thing about Bob?

If you weren't a painter then what do you think you would be?

As a painter, who is your favourite cartoon character? (Mickey Mouse etc)

Thank you very much,

Chappy Williams
Brought Ferry Correspondent

From: Colin Jackson
To: Bob Servant
Subject: Chappy

Hello Bob,

Your friend Chappy has sent me the questions for the newspaper. Do you want to answer them in a way that will suit you?

Colin

From: Bob Servant
To: Colin Jackson
Subject: Re: Chappy

Hello Colin,
That's all fine. just send the answers directly to Chappy. Speak to you later. I'm waiting for the woman at the post office to phone me back about this money transfer but she's probably doing her bloody nails or something.

Bob

From: Colin Jackson
To: Chappy Williams
Subject: ANSWERS

Thanks Chappy if you need more information on me you know how to get to me. Tell Bob that I am very grateful for this interview and i am looking forward to read the paper.

Thanks and have a nice day.

Colin

How long have you been an artist and what was it that made you start?

My Dad was an artist and I grow up living with my Dad. It became part of me but I can say that when I officially opened up to the world as a painter was in 1995 when I inherited his studio and became officially know as painter Colin...lol. So I will say that I have been a painter for about 12 years now.

Bob said that you think in pictures can you please explain this?

Well as a painter I actually think in pictures because everything I see around me I imagine them in painting and how they will look if they painted in pictures, so I really imagine a lot of things in paintings especially when I am at work in my studio. I think in pictures as Bob says.

 **DELETE THIS AT YOUR PERIL**

How did you meet Bob?

Well I met Bob on the internet while I was looking for a representative. Bob got my mail and replied asking to see some of my paintings. He grow interest in me and since then I and Bob have been good friends because he is fun talking to and also a caring fellow to know.

You are doing a painting of Bob in a boat, is it true that he was a captain in the Merchant Navy?

Yes I am doing a painting of Bob in Bob's Beauty. For as long as I have been talking to him I know him as Captain Bob because from the day I met him he told me he was a captain in the merchant navy and I believe he is a captain, so if I am asked if Bob is a captain I will say yes.

Do you think he is handsome?

Yes Bob must have been handsome when he was younger because he has worked hard in his jobs to earn a lot of money and so would have got fit along the way. With his good jokes also you can imagine how good he would been with women? I just think the skirts would have been on cue for Bob at his young days! Yes he is a handsome man!

What is your favourite thing about Bob?

My favourite thing about Bob is that he sounds like a good man and I am always pleased to read his mails because he is usually interesting in his writing. Bob must be fun being around.

If you weren't a painter then what do you think you would be?

I would have loved to be an international journalist.

As a painter, who is your favourite cartoon character?

My favourite cartoon is Tom and Jerry and Pink and the Brain.

From: Chappy Williams
To: Colin Jackson
Subject: Thank You

Thanks very much Colin,
I loved the Tom and Jerry joke! The story is all filed and I think it is

very funny.

I hope you and Bob enjoy it,

All the best,

Chappy

From: Bob Servant
To: Colin Jackson
Subject: TOM AND FUCKING JERRY?

Colin,
What are you playing at?! Have you seen the Telegraph? What were you thinking? I never said anything about Tom and Jerry, I don't even like the bloody programme.

   I've been getting absolute pelters all day. People keep giving it 'Ooh, Jerry, where's Colin?' And what's all this bollocks about you thinking I'm so handsome? We come across as a right couple of oddballs. By Christ, you've made me look like a complete idiot. Why the hell would I say that we're the new Tom and Jerry. What does that even mean, they were in a fucking cartoon for a start? I wouldn't know where to begin.

I am absolutely furious about this Colin.

Bob

DELETE THIS AT YOUR PERIL

Dundee Evening Telegraph

Broughty Ferry News

25·02·07

Filed 25.02.07 by Chappy Williams, Broughty Ferry Correspondent

WE'RE LIKE TOM AND JERRY, SAYS PAINTER ABOUT BROUGHTY FERRY MAN

An internationally known artist who has been commissioned by Broughty Ferry resident Bob Servant to produce a portrait has bizarrely claimed that the two of them believe they are the "new Tom and Jerry".

Colin Jackson, an English painter who was inspired by his father to pick up the brush back in the 1990s, contacted Servant through the Internet and the two of them hit it off immediately.

"I am always pleased to read Bob's emails", says Jackson, "Because he is usually interesting. Bob must have been a handsome young man because from the recent pictures he sent me he still looks great so you can imagine how good he would been if he was younger?"

It was while emailing each other about the painting, which is to show Servant on board a ship called 'Bob's Beauty' from his long career in the Merchant Navy, that Jackson claims the two of them decided that they could be the modern-day incarnation of Walt Disney's much loved cartoon duo.

"It was Bob's idea", says Jackson. "We both love Tom and Jerry and he suggested that we could make ourselves like them. He said the world is crying out for a new Tom and Jerry and we would be perfect for the job. I'm not sure how we're going to make ourselves the new Tom and Jerry because they were cartoon characters but, knowing Bob as I do, he'll have something up his sleeve!"

However, when contacted by the Evening Telegraph today, Servant claimed he had no knowledge of the Tom and Jerry plan. "This is news to me", he said from Doc Ferry's public bar[26].

---

26 This article is nowhere to be found in the records of the *Evening Telegraph* for the date given or, indeed, any date in the paper's history. I am very confident in declaring that it was Bob, and not Chappy Williams, who was the author of this piece of fiction.

DELETE THIS AT YOUR PERIL

From: Colin Jackson
To: Bob Servant
Subject: Re: TOM AND FUCKING JERRY?

Hello Bob,
Whats all this about? I only said I liked Tom and Jerry not you so I think your friend Williams should be confronted not me. So i don't see any reason why you should be harassing me like i am some kind of toy or something like that.

Colin

From: Bob Servant
To: Colin Jackson
Subject: I am sorry Colin but this is goodbye

Colin,
I have spoken to Chappy and he is sticking to his story. The last few days have been a complete nightmare and I have been turned into a laughing stock by the Tom and Jerry story. The local radio station had a phone-in yesterday on the matter and the resounding opinion was that I was a basket case.

A taxi driver phoned in from the Seagate rank in Dundee and said that he'd just seen me chasing a mouse down the road with a rubber hammer (which was untrue) and then a woman from Monifieth called and, sounding all pleased with herself, said, "Forget Walt Disney, I think Bob Servant's been on the Malt Whisky".

I knew things were bad when I nipped up to the bowling club and bumped into Jimmy Walker and Bill Wood. Jimmy went to shake my hand and then said, 'Hang on Bob, have you washed your paws?' Then Bill said that the bar was closed so would I be able to nip through the cat flap and get them a couple of drinks? They're both right good guys so when they have a pop you know you're in trouble.

I am sorry Thomas but under the circumstances I cannot take the painting from you. I just want to forget about the whole matter. I do not hold any grudge against you, it's just one of those things. Best of luck for the future,

Yours,

Bob Servant

No Reply

96   DELETE THIS AT YOUR PERIL

6

From Lanzhou to Willy's Chinese Palace

From: LANZHOU GLOBAL LTD
To: Bob Servant
Subject: JOB OPPORTUNITY/ MAKE MORE INCOME

Dear Sir/Madam,
We are Lanzhou Global, a specialist in the production of Rubber belts such as power transmission belts, conveyor belts etc. We have reached big sales volume of rubber products in USA/Canada and now trying to penetrate the United Kingdom and European market. Quite soon we shall open representative offices in the United Kingdom and therefore we are looking for people to assist us.

We need agents to receive payment in bank wire transfers and to resend the money to us. You earn 10% from each operation and work as an independent contractor right from your home office. Your job is absolutely legal. You can earn up to 3000-4000 pounds monthly.

Best Regards,

Admin/Human Resources Manager,
Xiong Li.

From: Bob Servant
To: LANZHOU GLOBAL LTD
Subject: OK, let's talk

Hello there
This looks very interesting indeed. My name is Bob Servant and I am a semi-retired window cleaner. How would I go about applying for this job?

Your Servant,

Bob Servant

From: LANZHOU GLOBAL LTD
To: Bob Servant
Subject: JOB OPPORTUNITY/ MAKE MORE INCOME

Dear Bob,
Thanks for responding to our offer. We are pleased with your interest. We are looking to extend our business to United Kingdom and have been facing difficulties in handling payments from our client, that is why we have decided to employ people over there whom we can trust. Do you understand our aims OK? Do not

  DELETE THIS AT YOUR PERIL

hesitate to ask any question.

XIONG LI

From: Bob Servant
To: LANZHOU GLOBAL LTD
Subject: MY GARAGE COULD BE AN OFFICE

Xiong,
I am very interested in working for your company. I have a big garage that I do not use much and I was thinking that I could convert it into an office? The only thing is that it is absolutely freezing in there because I knocked a hole in the wall once when I decided that I needed an escape tunnel from the house. Looking back it was a stupid decision but it was around the time of the Millennium Bug and a lot of people were panicking. I remember wee Jane at Mrs. Muffin's being too scared to use their till on New Year's Day because Chappy Williams told her it might explode.

There isn't much in the garage -just a bike, a barbecue and about 30,000 jazz mags.

Many thanks,

Bob

PS What would be my job title?

PPS Is there a uniform?

From: LANZHOU GLOBAL LTD
To: Bob Servant
Subject: Re: MY GARAGE COULD BE AN OFFICE

Hello Bob,
Thanks a lot. Listen Bob this job does not require your much time or space. It's lucrative but all we need is you handling and collecting payments from our clients.You do not need a uniform for this and get 10% of each payment. You can give yourself any title you want. Please give us your full personal and banking details so we can get started with this now Bob,

Thanks,

Xiong

From: Bob Servant
To: LANZHOU GLOBAL LTD
Subject: Thoughts on a uniform

Xiong,

I am an old-fashioned kind of man and as far as I'm concerned if you are working then you wear a uniform, it's as simple as that. Perhaps it would be possible for me to arrange a uniform over here and show you to see if it ties in with your corporate image? What kind of look do you go for yourself? Do you wear a suit or a branded tracksuit?

I want something tight, that's vital. It makes me feel alert. I remember when I still had the windowcleaning round. Whenever we had a bumper day I used to wear two pairs of pants, tight ones too and sometimes stick a dishcloth down there as well. I walked about the place like a bloody cowboy but it really put me in the zone. I remember the boys down at Toshy's Hardware used to encourage me. One time a few of them stuck me in the shop window and managed to get eight towels down my pants and trousers while everyone clapped outside[27].

With regards to the information you need about old Bob here, can you please be a bit more specific. I have had a long and fruitful life Xiong, and if I'm going to open that can of worms then God only knows what could pop out! Your new employee, a proud member of the Lanzhou Team,

The Big Man,

Bob Servant

From: LANZHOU GLOBAL LTD
To: Bob Servant
Subject: APPLICATION FORM

Hello Big Man!
We are glad to have you as our staff, this is the information that we need. Do what you think is best for a uniform Bob. We trust you. I wear a suit.

PERSONAL DETAILS

First Name:
Middle Name:
Last Name:

---

27 A quick call to Toshy's Hardware in Broughty Ferry unsurprisingly confirms that this incident did not take place.

DELETE THIS AT YOUR PERIL

Date Of Birth:
Sex:
Occupation:
Marital Status:
National Insurance Number/Social Security Number:
Address:

City:
State:
Zip/Postal Code:
Country:
Home Phone:
Mobile Phone:
Fax:

CERTIFICATION:
I hereby certify that all entries are true and complete. I agree and understand that any falsification of information, regardless of time of discovery, may cause forfeiture on my part of employment in the service of Lanzhou Global Manufacturing Co. Ltd. I consent to criminal history background checks.

Date:

Applicant Signature:

OFFICIAL USE ONLY:

Remarks:

Lanzhou Global Manufacturing Co., Ltd.

Thailand.

- - - - - - - - - - - - - - - -

From: Bob Servant
To: LANZHOU GLOBAL LTD
⁄ Subject: UNIFORMS

Xiong,
Hello boss! I have been trying like a bastard to find the right uniform for the job and I think I have it - a boilersuit that I bought for £30 from Nipper Kolacz, who works at the Michelin. Nipper wasn't able to give me a receipt because they get given them free but could I still claim it on expenses?

Here's what I want to do with it. On the front left chest pocket I want to put my initials - BGS - like what football managers have on their training jackets. It's on the back that I want to get a little bit saucy. I don't know if you have a slogan over there at LANZHOU GLOBAL LTD or not but I have come up with one that I think is a bit of a cracker.

Are you ready?

HEY DICKHEAD! ARE YOU LAUGHING AT OUR RUBBER? SHUT UP OR WE'LL BELT YOU!

(And then underneath that) - LANZHOU GLOBAL - THE BEST RUBBER BELTS IN THE WORLD.

What do you think? It's quite long so the writing would have to be pretty small but I think it sets the right tone. It's extremely funny but also presents us as a serious international rubber belt company.

One final thing, are we going to advertise the fact that we have touched down in Scotland? I was up in Fintry the other day looking for skirt and I saw a cracking advertising board. I took a photo of it to show you as I thought it would be a great spot for a LANZHOU GLOBAL LTD advert - maybe using my new slogan? Let me know what you think, it's got a car on it just now but it's not a real car so it would be easy to take it off.

I've really enjoyed my first two days of working for LANZHOU GLOBAL LTD. It's been all go, but I have had a great time. I'll get to grips with the form tomorrow.

This is Bob Servant, star man of Lanzhou Global Ltd, clocking off!

Yours loyally,

Barbara

DELETE THIS AT YOUR PERIL

From: LANZHOU GLOBAL LTD
To: Bob Servant
Subject: Form needed

Dear Bob,
I am glad to read your message, i am very impressed with you and i must say you might be one of our best staff because of your good attitude and loyalty. I am proud of you and i feel you can help us have a large market in the UK. The uniform sounds perfect. You should wear it when you are doing your business as you will look smart. Let us have a think about what advertisements we might do but you have made a good start.

Bob, do not hesitate to send back your job application form. It is very important and we need this information for our system. We also have clients that will start making payments into your banking account very soon,

XIONG

From: Bob Servant
To: LANZHOU GLOBAL LTD
Subject: Completed Form (stick it in your pipe and smoke it!) (only joking) (though you can if you want) (don't choke to death without paying me though!) (only joking)

Xiong,
I've done the form! Isn't this incredible Xiong, old Bobby boy working for a Chinese belt company?! But why not? The thing is Xiong, you're over there in China and I'm here in Broughty Ferry. But

you're just a man and I'm just a man. That's what I'm saying. We're all just men. Apart from women.

All the very, very best,

Sandra

JOB APPLICATION FORM
PERSONAL DETAILS

First Name: BOB
Middle Name: GODZILLA
Last Name: SERVANT

Date Of Birth: 62 YEARS OLD DO NOT CELEBRATE BIRTHDAY
                 BECAUSE OF STRESS OF ORGANISING PARTY

Sex: MALE (100%)

Occupation: SCOTTISH REPRESENTATIVE FOR LANZHOU
                 GLOBAL LTD

Marital Status: SINGLE/AVAILABLE

National Insurance Number/Social Security Number: WOULD
                 RATHER WORK CASH IN HAND PLEASE

Address: 18 HARBOUR VIEW
City: DUNDEE
State: TAYSIDE
Zip/Postal Code: ZIP?
Country: SCOTLAND

Home Phone: BROKEN
Mobile Phone: GOT ONE FOR CHRISTMAS FROM TOMMY
                 PEANUTS BUT LOST IN BET ON BOXING DAY
                 (ARM WRESTLE WITH TOMMY PEANUTS)[28]

Fax: I THINK THE POST OFFICE HAS ONE THAT I
                 COULD USE?

CERTIFICATION:

---

28 Bob does, in actual fact, possess a mobile phone that he calls 'The Batphone'. For the first six months he owned it, Bob used his phone only while standing in phone boxes after Chappy Williams told him that they were the only locations that offered a signal for his particular model.

  DELETE THIS AT YOUR PERIL

I hereby certify that all entries are true and complete. I agree and understand that any falsification of information, regardless of time of discovery, may cause forfeiture on my part of employment in the service of Lanzhou Global Manufacturing Co. Ltd. I consent to criminal history background checks.

Date: 28/3/07

Applicant Signature: **Bobby Servant**. By the way, about those checks, I smoked a few Fatty Boom Booms in the late 1970s but I never really enjoyed them that much. Other than that, you'll probably dig up some bits and pieces but they all resulted from genuine misunderstandings.

FOR OFFICIAL USE ONLY:

Remarks: BOB IS A GOOD GUY

From: LANZHOU GLOBAL LTD
To: Bob Servant
Subject : MISSING INFORMATION

Hello Bob,
Thank you for sending the form but it is not totally correct. You did not give us your postal address and no national insurance number. Kindly do that and meanwhile one of our clients is ready to make a payment so we need your phone number and bank details soon,

Thank You,

XIONG

From: Bob Servant
To: LANZHOU GLOBAL LTD
Subject: STAFF PARTY

Xiong,
Thanks you for your email. You know, Xiong, when I hear from you, my special boss with his kind words, I feel about ten feet tall. It's lucky I'm not though, or I wouldn't be able to get into my house! I would, of course, I could just crawl in the front door or lever myself through a window. Either way, I'd get into the house. That's for bloody sure.
     Xiong, I have been very, very busy. I know you want to get these forms done but it's not all about paperwork in business Xiong, you

DELETE THIS AT YOUR PERIL

should know that. What we need Xiong, is to let people know that we are here and we mean business. Rubber belt business.

I've started spreading the word locally in Broughty Ferry, and then I'll take it on a rolling campaign through Douglas and Mid Craigie, up the Kingsway and back through the West End to the city centre. People are intrigued and welcoming to the company and they're fascinated by where we want to take it.

I have also been thinking about a staff night out. Obviously, as things stand there is just me here in the Scottish office, but I was thinking of inviting a couple of people. The first guy I thought of was Clive from the Royal Bank[29]. Clive is a bit eccentric but is also quite senior I think. He's a good guy and he could be quite important to us for setting up bank accounts and so on. The other one is Hamish McAlpine, the former Dundee United goalkeeper. Hamish is a distinctive local character and a good guy to have onside. I have attached a photo.

With regards to locations, then I think that Chinese would be the most appropriate as I'm sure you agree! Ha, ha. Probably the best Chinese in Broughty Ferry is Willy's Chinese Palace. They do a good dinner deal for under a tenner so if Clive, Hamish and myself all have that and maybe two bottles of wine then you'd be talking about £40-£50 for the whole thing.

Is that OK? Shall I just keep a receipt and send it over to you?

Anyway, I'd better be off. I've got a major marketing plan for the next few days, which I will tell you about later. I'm hoping to surprise you with some great news.

Your Faithful Employee and Friend,

Bob Servant

From: LANZHOU GLOBAL LTD
To: Bob Servant
Subject: Information Bob

Bob,
Thank you again for your hard work for the company. I think that the

---

29 Bob originally refused to tell me if Clive exists. Having spent two days ascertaining that no Clive has ever worked at any Broughty Ferry bank, Bob then admitted he has never met anyone called Clive. He generously added that he does know a Cliff, a man who he describes as 'a total clown'.

  **DELETE THIS AT YOUR PERIL**

party is a good idea and yes we would prefer you to eat at a Chinese restaurant as we are a Chinese company originally. But Bob you have still not given us your national insurance number, bank account information and phone number right away. You said that Tommy broke your phone have you not got another one?

Also, we cannot find a record of your address, have you written it properly?

Please hurry Bob

Xiong

From: Bob Servant
To: LANZHOU GLOBAL LTD
Subject: Will the rain affect the belts?

Xiong,

My address is 18 Harbour View, Broughty Ferry. It's the house with the long grass, next but one to the house with the greenhouse. That's Frank Theplank's house. You might have heard that he used to work with me at a cafe I had but the whole thing turned to shit. We're back talking now but for a while it was purely nods and winks.

I do have a National Insurance number, it is ▬▬▬▬. However, I would really not want to get the Government involved in this whole kettle of Chinese fish. I have not paid any taxes since '89 and that was by mistake and because I was sitting pretty from the cheese burger vans and half-mad at the time.

Unfortunately I do not have a phone right now. A few months ago I went absolutely berserk on Booty Express but it turned out it was costing me £1 a bloody minute. I couldn't believe it, I thought they were joking when they said that stuff at the beginning of the call. The girls were quality, Xiong, real good time girls with very few hang-ups. We had some great times but then I got the bill through and it was nearly £300. One thing led to another and I took out the phone with a spanner.

Do you want me to get a new one for the business? There's a nice one in the Argos Catalogue for £8.99 but my Argos Catalogue is three years old so you can probably stick a fiver on top of that.

Things have been going really well with getting people talking about the business. One thing though, a lot of people are excited but ask me the same question - What do the rubber belts look like and how much are they going to cost? There is some resistance from the usual suspects. In the Post Office bar the other day Chappy Williams said, "Why would I wear a rubber belt Bob, I'd look like a prick" and then, in The Anchor, Tommy Peanuts said that rubber belts would shrink in the rain and cut off the circulation to your legs.

I thought that was a fair point actually, is it true?

By the way, the staff party is booked for Willy's Chinese Palace. I nipped in earlier and reserved a table for three, and Hamish and Clive are both confirmed. Chick Devine, the barman at Stewpot's, is cousins with Hamish and says he'll definitely be there. I went to the bank and confirmed with Clive as well. He went all weird, bright red and saying how excited he was and stuff. He's a weirdo, I hope he's not going to be an idiot at the party.

Your best worker,

Bob Servant

From: LANZHOU GLOBAL LTD
To: Bob Servant
Subject: Thank you Bob

Bob,
How are you? Thank you for the information. We are now going to set up the first payment to you of £3,000. You can take £300 commission from this as reward for all your hard work. You can also take the money for the party at Willy's Palace. We would like you to have a good time at the party so will pay what you need in extra commission.

So now Bob we just need your bank information. Please send this so I can have everything set up,

Thanks you and well done,

Xiong

From: Bob Servant
To: LANZHOU GLOBAL LTD
Subject: PARTY TIME FOR LANZHOU!

Xiong,
Well, this is it, the day of the LANZHOU GLOBAL LIMITED (SCOTLAND) staff night out. I am so excited Xiong. The last staff party I went to was when I still had the windowcleaning round and I took the boys up to Godden's Goodtime Girls in Dundee for some tabledancing. Christ, that was a disaster. The two women that came out looked as if they were the bloody cleaners and they were so clumsy about everything it was hard to relax. In fact, now I come to think of it, they might well have been the cleaners. It was only half past ten in the morning.

  **DELETE THIS AT YOUR PERIL**

I remember when we got back down the Ferry we told Father O'Neill about it and he was pissing himself laughing, joking about how he was going to take the church mob there for their Christmas do. He's a good guy Father O'Neill. He always gets his round in and he's honest too. He once admitted to me and Tommy Peanuts that the Bible's a lot of bollocks and he's only in the game for the free accomodation[30].

Anyway, I'm sure tonight will be a big success. I popped my head through the door at Stewpot's and shouted over to Chick Devine if Hamish was definitely going to be there. He said "Yeah, that's right Bob, Hamish McAlpine's going to your party" and everyone laughed, but that's just because they're jealous.

Listen, Xiong, I am going to speak to Clive at the party about the banking needs for LANZHOU GLOBAL. What kind of account do I need? I'm not bothered, as long as I get one of those plastic card holders. Tommy Peanuts has one and he's forever flashing it about. The way he lets the thing fall open at the bar you'd think he was from the fucking FBI.

Your faithful employee and one of your best friends,

Daphne

From: LANZHOU GLOBAL LTD
To: Bob Servant
Subject: RE: PARTY TIME FOR LANZHOU!

Hello BOB,
We are a little concerned as we checked your name and address on the UK directory online but we could not find it. So how do we know you are whom you claim to be? Also this is no joke, this is a job offer and we want you to take it serious. We have clients who want to make payment with cheque and balance transfer but we are afraid that it seems the details you gave is incorrect and you are not taking us serious.

We hope you are not a joke Bob. Kindly mail back.

XIONG

---

30 I should clarify that the figure of 'Father O'Neill' is not based on any past or present representative of any religious organisation, in Broughty Ferry or elsewhere.

From: Bob Servant
To: LANZHOU GLOBAL LTD
Subject: Party, Address

Xiong,

I have some bad news, which I will come to shortly, but first I want to voice my deep anger. Xiong, are you calling me a liar? The only way that business can work is with 100% honesty and that is what I have given you.

I am ex-directory because five years ago I stole a wheelbarrow and several potted plants from Dawson Park. I was worried that the council were cahoots with BT for stuff like that so went ex-directory. I wish you had asked what was going on rather than jump to conclusions and try me in a kangaroo court. You are behaving like Adolf Hitler. That said, I entirely forgive you.

I do, however, have bad news. The party was a disaster. First, Hamish McAlpine didn't turn up. It turns out Chick Devine doesn't know Hamish at all. He's a stupid liar who thinks he's funny. The only thing that made me think they're cousins is that Chick has a moustache as well but that doesn't really mean anything does it? Especially when you look at the fact I've never seen Chick and Hamish together and that they don't look alike. And that Chick's black.

So, anyway, Hamish didn't show and Clive totally misunderstood the whole thing and thought me and him were going on some sort of bloody date. Xiong, the guy turned up in a fucking dress and make-up. I walked in and thought there was no-one there apart from some rough bird and then looked again and it was actually Clive. I had brought along a few belts and a speech but it was all a waste of time. Clive started nicking all the prawn crackers and things got a bit out of hand.

The police came, which was a total overreaction. Someone grassed to the Evening Telegraph and they (surprise, surprise) stuck it in today. I've been getting pelters about what happened and all the stuff with Clive. Everyone keeps asking me where my boyfriend is and if I'm off up to the bank to kiss him. I popped into Stewpot's for lunch and the boys in there gave it - 'Oooh, did Clive let you open his account Bob' and 'Don't be jealous Bob, but I was up the bank earlier and I caught Clive fiddling with some coppers'.

That last one made me laugh to be honest. Then Chappy Williams got in trouble trying to do something with 'overdrafts'. It was brilliant. He said, 'Ooh did Clive give you an overdraft Bob?' and I just said, 'How's that funny Chappy?' and everyone laughed at him, so that was not too bad. I just finished my pie and left after that.

Anyway, I'll attach the article. They've always had it in for me, ever since I was interviewed on Radio Tay at the Broughty Ferry gala week and the reporter asked if I read about the Evening Telegraph saying the gala week was the worst ever and I said that I only ever

DELETE THIS AT YOUR PERIL

bought the Evening Telegraph if the Spar has sold out of toilet paper. It wasn't my joke (It was one of Frank Theplanks though, when he said it, I'm not sure if he was joking)[31]. The paper have been on my back ever since. They're always throwing in the thing about my ladders being nicked and how it wasn't gypsies that stole them. It definitely was.

Your loyal employee,

Bob Servant

PS here's the article –

Dundee Evening Telegraph
Broughty Ferry News
28·03·07

Filed 01.04.07 by Broughty Ferry Breaking News Team

Chinese Company's Christmas Night Out Ends in Farcical Scenes

Chaos reigned at a Broughty Ferry restaurant last night when two local men celebrated a Christmas night out that ended with one of them tying the other to a postbox and force-feeding him prawn crackers. The victim, who was dressed in women's clothing and has asked not to be named, required medical treatment at the scene by paramedics in what police described today as, "a moment of madness" from the attacker, Robert Servant (62) of Harbour View Road.

The night, sponsored by Chinese company Lanzhou Global Development Ltd, for whom Mr Servant is Director of Operations (Scotland), got off to a bizarre beginning according to witnesses. When Mr Servant arrived at Willy's Chinese Palace restaurant in Gray Street, he was "astonished" to see his fellow diner sitting waiting for him, according to manager Willie Yuan.

"Mr Servant, who we have had trouble with before, went berserk", said Mr. Yuan this morning. "He started shouting, 'what the hell's up with your get up?', 'why are you wearing a f***ing dress?' And then he was saying, 'Where's Hamish? Where's Hamish?' It was very frightening indeed and it was a relief when he finally sat down".

The staff say they were too

---

31 After an exhaustive search of Radio Tay's transcripts for every Broughty Ferry Gala Week for the past twenty years, no record of this conversation can be found. I confidently state that the *Evening Telegraph* made no such claim about the much-admired Broughty Ferry Gala Week, and Bob Servant made no such claim about his less-admired bottom.

DELETE THIS AT YOUR PERIL

scared to tackle Mr Servant who then proceeded to dine in silence with his companion, a situation seemingly ended when Mr Servant felt that he had been cheated out of his share of the communal bowl of prawn crackers.

"That was when things got completely out of hand", said Mr Yuan. "The two of them started shouting and fighting and it spilled out onto the street. Mr Servant seemed to have a number of men's belts with him and he used these to tie his friend to the postbox. Then he ran back in and stole some bags of prawn crackers and went back outside".

"We locked the doors but we could see him stuffing the crackers into his friend's mouth and that's when we called the police. He was shouting 'Happy now? Happy now?' It was terrifying, I told the waiter to close the curtains and we didn't open them until we heard the sirens".

Mr Servant was arrested at the scene but later released when the victim of the attack refused to press charges. A police spokesman today confirmed that Mr Servant was known to them and his future behaviour would be observed. Mr Servant was not available for comment and his house showed little signs of life while Lanzhou Global Development Ltd could not be traced at the time of going to press[32].

From: LANZHOU GLOBAL LTD
To: Bob Servant
Subject: I am sorry Bob

Hello Bob,
I am very sorry. I am only doing my job and asking you the questions that the company's personnel manager is telling me to ask you. I know that you are OK Bob, but they have told me to ask. We need to know if the details given to us are for real.

A client wants to make payment with balance transfer. You know what this is? So he needs your credit card long number and the limit so he can make the payment on it. Also can i know which bank you use? I know there is now a problem with Clive so let me know what bank you will use.

Do not worry about the party. Sometimes when men are together things happen that no-one is proud of. The newspaper will forget about it I am sure as have the police. That is more important as you cannot work for us in jail!

---

32 After a slightly less taxing search, it can be established that this article never appeared in the *Evening Telegraph*.

DELETE THIS AT YOUR PERIL

Thanks

Xiong

From: Bob Servant
To: LANZHOU GLOBAL LTD
Subject: IT'S OVER

Xiong,
My friend. I hope that you can see my reasons for saying what I am about to say. We've had some good times together. We've laughed and joked and worked damn hard to get LANZHOU GLOBAL LTD the respect that it undoubtedly deserves. I love the company Xiong and, in many ways, I love you.But things change my friend. Sometimes life just grabs you by the balls and whispers 'think again compadre' whilst stroking your neck.

Xiong, I'll be honest with you, I'm holding up my hands and taking on the long walk. I know what you might think, that old Bob here has lost his bottle. That ten years ago Bob Servant would have turned round to the critics of LANZHOU GLOBAL LTD and told them to shut it, that we were going to show them we meant business and that, come the summer, every man and his dog in Dundee would be wearing one of our rubber belts. And you know what, Xiong, maybe you'd be right. Maybe you'd be right.

It's the paper Xiong, the bloody paper. That's what whored it for us. They just kept on my bloody back, coming round and ringing the bell and shouting 'come on Mr Servant, we only want a quick word'. But they didn't just want a quick word Xiong. They wanted their pound of flesh and, this afternoon, I suppose that's just what they got.

I was down at the Fisherman's Bar when I heard that they were in a bidding war with the Gazette for Clive's side of the story, 'My Chinese Horror' that he was demanding £25 for. I don't think he would have gone through with it. He doesn't have the guts and would have had to live in hiding somewhere I wouldn't track him down. Invergowrie, or even through in Perth.

Anyway, I decided that enough was enough. I spoke to Pop Wood who told me that legally, the best advice he could give me was to 'see the thing off at the pass' and speak to the Evening Telegraph myself. Pop is a great lawyer, though he's struck off for giving a false alibi to Tommy Peanuts when he vandalised Sally Peanut's new husband's Renault Laguna outside Maciocia's chip shop. That's why he's in the Fisherman's all the time I suppose.

So I called up the Evening Telegraph vipers and told them to come down. We cleaned the dominoes table and stuck it in the beer garden. Pop gave me a tie that he had in his briefcase (he carries it all the time because his wife doesn't know he's been struck off). I put on his glasses but they gave me a sore head so I took them off. I made a little sign out of the back of one of the menus and wrote 'BOB SERVANT STRIKES BACK' on it and propped it up in front of me.

Then I sat and composed myself with a gin and juice while Pop waited in the bar. I could hear him say 'Mr Servant will see you now' and he led the journalist through to the beer garden. Things went not too badly, I attach the article below. They managed to get in the thing about the ladders, which I knew they would, but they didn't really twist my words like the press can.

And that's that I suppose Xiong. I'd like to place on record how much I have enjoyed my time working with LANZHOU GLOBAL LTD. We've had a great wee spell and I have certainly done what I can to spread word throughout the Dundee area. At the very least Xiong, people will give you a chance.

I suppose this is goodbye Xiong. Oh, God, I can't believe I'm writing these words. I'm going to stop now before I begin to cry. I will never, ever forget you.

God Bless Xiong and God Bless LANZHOU GLOBAL LTD.

Your ex-employee but lifelong friend.

I love you Xiong, you were more than a boss,

Bob 'Xiong' Servant

Dundee Evening Telegraph
Broughty Ferry News   30·03·07

Filed 03.04.07 by Broughty Ferry Breaking News Follow-up Squad

Broughty Ferry Man Cuts Ties with Chinese Firm

A Broughty Ferry man who recently sparked havoc in a local restaurant has announced that he is cutting all ties with the Chinese firm that sponsored the evening and had been rumoured to be considering a major financial investment in the Dundee area.

Robert Servant (62) says that, though he has had "the time of his life", since taking a senior position with the company, Lanzhou Global Ltd, he feels it "is in the best interests of everyone", that they go their separate ways.

"I was approached by Lanzhou a couple of weeks ago now", said Mr Servant this afternoon during an impromptu press conference in the beer

DELETE THIS AT YOUR PERIL

garden of The Fishermens' Public Bar, "and they gave me a really terrrific post. Basically, the company makes rubber belts and we hoped that we would see a lot of people in Dundee making the switch from leather to rubber and so on".

"It could have been a great thing for Dundee and it was exciting to be involved", added Mr Servant, who is being unofficially represented by disgraced local lawyer Mike 'Pop' Wood. "There was then a bit of a mix-up at the staff night out (Mr Servant was involved in an altercation that resulted in both the police and ambulance services being called to Willy's Chinese Palace in Gray Street) and I really think that it may have soiled the whole project".

"More to the point, it has come to my attention that rubber belts are not big sellers. Quite frankly, we did not get the interest that we would have hoped. I think, and I'm not just talking about rubber belts, people should not be so scared of trying new things. I think in ten years time we'll all be wearing rubber belts but that won't make me sad. In fact, it would make me happy because it would shut up the boo boys".

Mr Servant says he is now thinking about returning to the window cleaning business, which he quit in disgust after having his ladders stolen in 1996. At the time, Mr Servant spoke in the Evening Telegraph of his "certainty" that the ladders had been stolen by the travelling community. Tayside Police responded that there were no travellers in the Dundee area over that period[33].

From: LANZHOU GLOBAL LTD
To: Bob Servant
Subject: Re: IT'S OVER

Hi
How are you? I know from the start you are a clown, i laugh a lot when i read from you, you are such a joker.

From: Bob Servant
To: LANZHOU GLOBAL LTD
Subject: That's the spirit!

Hello there,
Good to hear from you. Yes, I was pulling your leg. I'm glad that you

---

33 If needed I can confirm that this article is, yet again, a fabrication by Bob. As was the described press conference in the Fishermans' Bar.

also enjoyed the whole thing. I'm just a fun guy really champ, and enjoy having a nice glass of cheap wine and getting on the old email. It's a hobby I suppose.

All the very best with the old 'Lanzhou' line. If you don't mind me saying so, I think it needs a little bit of polishing. Tell me, where are you from and do many people actually fall for this stuff?

Stay strong,

Bob Servant

From: LANZHOU GLOBAL LTD
To: Bob Servant
Subject: re: That's the spirit!

Hello Bob,
Of course many people do fall for it, you know lots of gimimicks now and you make your cash. If you also have anything to tell me let me know. I am from malaysia, tell me more about you.

From: Bob Servant
To: LANZHOU GLOBAL LTD
Subject: CHEERS

Hello there sport,
Well, you're a right little scamp with the thieving and that but I have to say I don't think you're a bad wee chap at heart.

Keep your nose clean you little tinker,

Farewell,

Bob

No Reply

 **DELETE THIS AT YOUR PERIL**

7
Bobby and Benjamin are New Friends

From: Benjamin Suma
To: Bob Servant
Subject: INVESTMENT PROPOSAL WITH URGENT ATTENTION

Dear Friend,
I am Benjamin, the son of Asbenjamin, a Military General from Sierra Leone. I hope the purpose of my reason and my present situation will be understood by you. At the point of his death my father directed me with instruction to take over the transfer of the box that contains the fund amounted to 20 millions U.S. dollars.

Based on this I decided to source for a neutral person that can assist me in working on the necessary arrangement. Your assistance shall be compensated with a percentage from the fund. I wait for your reply,

Yours Faithfully,

Benjamin

From: Bob Servant
To: Benjamin Suma
Subject: INTERESTING

I like the cut of your jib.

Your Servant,

Bob Servant

From: Benjamin Suma
To: Bob Servant
Subject: Please try to read carefully and understand...

Dear Mr Bob,
Thanks for your quick response. I want to tell you that i will give you 25% of the total money for all the assistance that require of you to do for me. I will like you to let me know your satisfaction about the offer? The security company where the fund is being deposited does not know the content of the box that contain the fund they were told that the box contains family valuable items.

Regards,

Benjamin

  **DELETE THIS AT YOUR PERIL**

From: Bob Servant
To: Benjamin Suma
Subject: Africa

Tell me about Africa my friend, is it as beautiful as they say?

Bob

From: Benjamin Suma
To: Bob Servant
Subject: Reply to this mail please

Well, life in Africa is not the same from country to country and from individual too. I don't really understand the motive of your question, could you be more specific? you have not also response to my mail? can i reach you on phone? I will need your contact and bank details to make things move.

I await your reply,

Benjamin

From: Bob Servant
To: Benjamin Suma
Subject: Hello

Benjamin,
I have heard many times of the African sunset, mostly from Tommy Peanuts but he's claiming to have seen it through binoculars when he was in Tenerife, which sounds a bit ridiculous to me? Oh, I want to be there with you in Africa Benjamin. Watching the sunset. Holding hands. I know, I know, I'm just a silly old woman. Why would you want to watch a sunset with me? You have your whole life ahead of you.

Bob

From: Benjamin Suma
To: Bob Servant
Subject: Reply please

I never knew you were a woman Bob. Don't say you are silly, everyone has to live as he or she pleases, this is my believe. Yes you are right there is a wonderful sunset in Africa. I will be happy to

DELETE THIS AT YOUR PERIL   119

watch with you and take you to interesting sites depends on your interest. Start drawing your plans to come down! meanwhile what about the other discussion? You have your contact and bank information for me Bob?

Regards,

Benjamin

From: Bob Servant
To: Benjamin Suma
Subject: Benjamin

Benjamin,
Oh, are you teasing me? Please, are you a handsome man? Something you should know Benjamin, is that I am a very beautiful woman. For years, I have had men chasing me down the street, trying to touch my knockers and that, but I have never been interested. I want something different than the silly men here in Scotland. I want a real man, an exciting man, someone who is tough and not afraid to cry.

Bobby

From: Benjamin Suma
To: Bob Servant
Subject: Reply

Bobby,
I am not teasing, this is how i see life am glad to know that you are a beautiful woman. I am a handsome man, strong and caring, we were brought bold. I start having a feeling that we could make something good out of REAL LOVE, if it is what we call it. Could you tell me more? I love to be direct, I hate been pretending,

Benjamin

From: Bob Servant
To: Benjamin Suma
Subject: Take it easy

Benjamin,
Please, slow down. I do like you, but you are moving too fast,

120   **DELETE THIS AT YOUR PERIL**

Bobby

PS What are you wearing?

From: Benjamin Suma
To: Bob Servant
Subject: Reply Please

A SHIRT AND JEENS

From: Bob Servant
To: Benjamin Suma
Subject: OK

Benjamin,
It's a classic combo. Thank you, I am just trying to get a picture of
you in my head. It is late now, time for me to go for my beauty sleep.
Do you have this saying in Africa? "Time for the beauty sleep".

Bobby Sleep

From: Benjamin Suma
To: Bob Servant
Subject: Reply to this

Thanks i hope you have a nice rest. Here we say nice rest, I think
both nice and beauty make the same!

Regards

Benjamin

From: Bob Servant
To: Benjamin Suma
Subject: Morning

Hello Benjamin,
I slept sensationally. What have you got planned for today? I'm
going to nip down the shop and buy some lovely ham to try and
cheer myself up. I'm feeling really sad today Benjamin, can you
cheer me up? Do you know any good jokes?

Bobby

From: Benjamin Suma
To: Bob Servant
Subject: Have a nice day

Yeah, why position yourself am going to make you happy today? You will like it don't tell me you are not feeling it? You can only tell me to slow down, which I will agree because I will hate to hurt you.

Last week I overheard a true story from one guy telling his friend, the guy just wedded, but two days before the wedding he went to meet his old girlfriend, but unfortunately after the night he mistakingly exchange his pant to the girl. He got home and slept, in the morning as he went out of the room, the wife to be saw the pant and alarm! Put yourself in a position of man, if it happen to you what would you do!

pls cheers up there I have made you happy?

From: Bob Servant
To: Benjamin Suma
Subject: A Real Belter

Benjamin,
That is a wonderful joke, thank you so much, it has really cheered me up. Why did the man put on the wrong pants?! What a silly man. It really is a funny joke. And, yes, you are right, I am feeling that there is something between us. But I don't want to rush things because then it might all turn to shit.

I think I'm going to go and watch a couple of James Bond films. Are you like James Bond Benjamin? He is my dream man. I think Connery probably gets my vote. Not just because he's Scottish and not English though. If you start thinking like that you end up with no teeth like Jocky Wilson[34].

Bobby

From: Benjamin Suma
To: Bob Servant
Subject: Hello

---

34 Some overdue accuracy from Bob here. Scottish former world darts champion Jocky Wilson lost his last tooth at the age of 28 due to an aversion to brushing his teeth. In a newspaper interview in the 1980s, Wilson explained this was due to his grandmother informing him as a young child that, 'the English poison the water'.

DELETE THIS AT YOUR PERIL

Darling, it happen in the night it was the lady's pant! I have am not watching Bonds these days. I love adventurous films, people like Michael Douglas, Kathleen Tuners, Devito.

From: Bob Servant
To: Benjamin Suma
Subject: Who had the pants on?

Benjamin,
So who was wearing the pants? The man?
　　Have you seen Romancing the Stone? Douglas, Turner, Devito. The old gang back together.

Bobby

From: Benjamin Suma
To: Bob Servant
Subject: Have a Nice Day

Morning dear,
The man is the one that wear the lady's pant the lady two wears the guy pant!
　　Yes i have seen the romancing the stone, the jewel of the nile, ruthless people, other people's money!

cheers

From: Bob Servant
To: Benjamin Suma
Subject: Quiz

Hello Benjamin,
Yes, I am good thanks. They are all wonderful films, and extremely well acted. I think I've seen a book called Other People's Money, about some fraudster guy. I can't believe they named it after a Danny Devito film, what a bunch of fannies. Do you know who this man is? You must do?

Bobby

DELETE THIS AT YOUR PERIL

From: Benjamin Suma
To: Bob Servant
Subject: Have a nice day

I wouldn't know him poor me. Can you put me through?

From: Bob Servant
To: Benjamin Suma
Subject: It's Ralphie

Hello Benjamin,
It's Ralphie Milne, the former Dundee United player. Do you mind
when women talk about football Benjy? Whenever I try and speak to
the men in the bars here about it they say that I only watch football
for the legs! I can't bloody win!
   Oh Benjamin, I'm very excited, my friend has just called me and
asked if I want to go to a party! What should I wear? I can't decide
whether to dress in something to get the boys excited or if I should
wear something fun.

Bobby

From: Benjamin Suma
To: Bob Servant
Subject: The Fun one

Bobby, wear something fun! You have an excited boy here that is all
you wish for! I wish you a good luck, am not going out. Yes you can
talk soccer. Will be thinking of you,

Benjamin

From: Bob Servant
To: Benjamin Suma
Subject: Ooh my head!

Benjamin,
How are my dear? Aargh, my head is so sore! I drank too much wine
at the party because I was so hot. The only fun outfit I had was a
rabbit costume and it was absolutely roasting. Do you know any
good hangover cures?

Bobby

  DELETE THIS AT YOUR PERIL

From: Benjamin Suma
To: Bob Servant
Subject: Have a nice day

Darling,
Once a while, it is good to satisfy one like that. Please drink a lot of water, or you top it with the same brand of drink.

I hope it really fun?

From: Bob Servant
To: Benjamin Suma
Subject: Good Idea

Thank you Benjamin, I will try that.

I have an idea, let's write a poem together. It's what lovers do in my country, one line at a time.

I'll start -

Bobby and Benjamin are new friends...

Now you write your line! It's fun!

Bobby x

From: Benjamin Suma
To: Bob Servant
Subject: so funful!

So lovely darling. Am working on some arrangement that will surely be of great blessing to our RELATIONSHIP! Am right about using this word? So nice an idea, so funful, ok my first line and second line.

YES BENJAMIN AND BOBBY HAVE JUST STARTED SOMETHING SO GREAT,

HOW SWEET WILL IT BE IF IT CAN BE BUILD WELL IN A SOLID FOUNDATION!

From: Bob Servant
To: Benjamin Suma
Subject: Lovely stuff

Here we go you big sausage -

Even though they live in very distant nations...

Can't wait to see your new line, your others have been ok, but maybe try and make it ryhme?

Bobby x

From: Benjamin Suma
To: Bob Servant
Subject: Benjamin and Bobby poem

Bobby and Benjamin are new friends,
Yes Benjamin and Bobby have just started something so great,
How sweet will it be if it can be build well in a solid foundation!
Even though they live in very distant nations
Yes this shouldn't count since they have strong feeling...

Benjamin x

From: Bob Servant
To: Benjamin Suma
Subject: Very nice

Maybe one day they will live together in Ealing...

From: Benjamin Suma
To: Bob Servant
Subject: Benjamin and Bobby poem

Bobby and Benjamin are new friends,
Yes Benjamin and Bobby have just started something so great,
How sweet will it be if it can be build well in a solid foundation!
Even though they live in very distant nations
Yes this shouldn't count since they have strong feeling
Maybe one day they will live together in Ealing
Very possible if really they both wish..

126   **DELETE THIS AT YOUR PERIL**

From: Bob Servant
To: Benjamin Suma
Subject: Last bit

I wonder if Benjamin likes fish?

From: Benjamin Suma
To: Bob Servant
Subject: Benjamin and Bobby poem

Bobby and Benjamin are new friends,
Yes Benjamin and Bobby have just started something so great,
How sweet will it be if it can be build well in a solid foundation!
Even though they live in very distant nations
Yes this shouldn't count since they have strong feeling
Maybe one day they will live together in Ealing
Very possible if really they both wish
I wonder if Benjamin likes fish?
Yes he like eating fish so much this days!

From: Bob Servant
To: Benjamin Suma
Subject: Ok that'll do

OK Benjamin, that'll do us there.

Well done, what a wonderful poem. I had a great day today. My friend Carol came round to the house and we washed my car together and made it look all pretty. I have attached a photo of Carol larking about on the car. I was going to get her to take a photo of me to send you but I am too shy!! I am worried that you won't think I am beautiful.

Bobby x[35]

---

35 At this point, Bob supplied a photo of a woman dancing on a car bonnet
   and holding a bottle of OVD rum. I contacted this woman, whose name I
   will certainly not reveal, and she made it quite clear that the photo was not
   to be used in the book. It was a moment of madness, she explained, after
   she got chatting to Bob in the queue at Woolworth's.

From: Benjamin Suma
To: Bob Servant
Subject: cheers

Whoa! Darling you have share your today joy with me! I can't wait to see your picture, i will love it don't worry. WHOM DO YOU DREAM ABOUT?

One day you will drive me, or won't you? (Bobby, i have one thing in my character I don't like people that doubt about what take their time.) I love it what is the car name? Thank you for brighting this joy. (Bobby, i have one thing in my character i dont like people that doubt on what they do).

I am working on an exciting business model for us that will help our future, my dear. It will need a little investment but not so much,

Benji

From: Bob Servant
To: Benjamin Suma
Subject: Test

Benjamin,
Hello my darling, thank you for your kind words. The car is called HOTPOT. Benjamin, Carol told me that I should give you a 'gentleman's test'. It's three questions and you have to say what you would do in these situations -

1. We are in a bar and another woman comes over and asks you to kiss her or touch her knockers. What do you do?

2. I am in HOTPOT and I wipe out an entire flock of sheep because I'm doing my lipstick. What do you do?

3. I eat a lot of lovely ham and get very, very fat. What do you do?

Bobby x

From: Benjamin Suma
To: Bob Servant
Subject: Gentleman test indeed

OK my answer

I will honestly never response to any other woman kisses when am with you

DELETE THIS AT YOUR PERIL

I have to stand by you under any situation as long as i love you, not only when it happen in my present but even in my absent. If this happens with HOTPOT I would help you as I could.

Yes, a change in your look will never have any effect in my love for you as long as i love you.

So what about the photo?

From: Bob Servant
To: Benjamin Suma
Subject: Dreamboat

Oh Benjamin,

You are wonderful. I am so nervous about sending you my photo! I do not have the courage yet. Please, can you send your one first? That would make me feel a lot better. I am so excited about seeing you, and showing you off to Carol and the rest of the girls! In the meantime, what is your favourite animal? I am generally lion mad but I also have a soft spot for the Australian kangaroo.

Bobby x

From: Benjamin Suma
To: Bob Servant
Subject: AM I CORRECT?

Dear,

My best animal is DOG I have one called Sharp. Am already having a feeling I can't express. I will send photo as soon as it is possible for me to do the scanning. Meanwhile, there is something that worries me. I seem to have told you much about me but you never say anything or you are not clear? You are interested in the business I mention?

Benjamin

From: Bob Servant
To: Benjamin Suma
Subject: My House

Benjamin,

I cannot wait to see the photo. I know that it will make me feel as if my heart is, quite literally, on fire. Well, what else do you want to know about me? I get upset when people are cruel to animals, or when I drop some of my lovely ham on the kitchen floor or I can't get my hair to look nice.

Talking about the old 'Badger's Lair' (hair), I am going to go to the hairdresser's at the weekend to get my hair looking nice and pretty for when I have my photo taken for sending to you. I hope you like it!

Bobby x

From: Benjamin Suma
To: Bob Servant
Subject: DO YOU BELIEVE

Bobby,
Would you be hurt if I ask this question. Are you serious with me? Do you believe in love, I mean real love BETWEEN MAN AND WOMAN? I think to love means that one might need to sacrifice? Things like money?

Benjamin

From: Bob Servant
To: Benjamin Suma
Subject: I see what you mean

Benjamin,
Yes, I believe that love means many sacrifices. God knows I found that out with my last boyfriend. He was a nasty man that used to call me names. He used to say that I was mental and that he wasn't my boyfriend, he was just my next-door neighbour and that I wasn't even a woman! He was an idiot, I'm glad he's not my boyfriend any more. He used to say 'stop messing about Bob, you're scaring me'. He was called Frank and he was a real hunk.

Where is your photo?

Bobby x

From: Benjamin Suma
To: Bob Servant
Subject: My Picture

Darling,
Am very sorry keeping you waiting pls tell me you are not offended. This picture was taken by the beach. I waiting eagerly to

  DELETE THIS AT YOUR PERIL

read from you,

Benjamin

From: Bob Servant
To: Benjamin Suma
Subject: You take me breath away

Benjamin,
You are incredible! The way you are sitting there, it's just great.
You're saying, "Yes, I'm on the beach, I'm relaxed, but I'm also

serious. I am sitting here and thinking about Bobby, and what she might be doing right now. I wonder how she is? I think I'll email her later and say hi. Ooh, it's hot here on the beach. Would anyone like an ice cream? I like ice cream a lot, especially the mint choc chip. I'm Benjamin, and I want to be covered in ice cream".

Those sunglasses - they make you look like a film star.

WELCOME TO THE BEACH

STARRING BENJAMIN SUMA

Do you know what I mean?

Bobby x

From: Benjamin Suma
To: Bob Servant
Subject: SO FUN

So joyful and loveable darling, thanks, you are a great imaginator!

I missed you a lot yesterday. I never seen you but you seem to have taken my whole lot of feeling! Well, we both better work hard to make it real and make happiness.

pls tell me something? Are you interested in business?

CHEERS

From: Bob Servant
To: Benjamin Suma
Subject: Question

Benjamin,
Have you ever heard of a clap-o-meter? They used to be on game shows all the time but not so much now. They're machines that measure audience applause. I wondered, would you be able to make one for me?

Bobby x

From: Benjamin Suma
To: Bob Servant
Subject: URGENT

Bobby, good day, how are you today? Yes i will surely be glad to

  **DELETE THIS AT YOUR PERIL**

make one if i know how to. Bobby you promised, your picture? Your thoughts please on business?

From: Bob Servant
To: Benjamin Suma
Subject: The Clap-O-Meter

Benjamin,
I was hoping you would say that. I can't wait to see what you come up with. Can you make sure it works off the same batteries as my television remote please? I buy them in boxes of fifty from Nipper Kolacz.

I have been sitting staring at your photo for hours on end - you look so mysterious in those sunglasses.

It's as if you are saying, "I'm Benjamin, and I'm a man to be reckoned with. I'm wearing sunglasses because it's sunny but also because it makes me mysterious, a bit like a cowboy. Maybe one day I'll move to the desert and be a cowboy. All day long I'll ride my horse and then go back to Bobby's house and she will have cooked me some lovely ham and potatoes and we'll eat all the ham and potatoes and then we'll go and sit down on the couch and watch The Antiques Roadshow and do each other's hair".

Was that more or less what you were thinking at the time? Oh, Benji, what are we going to do with you? You're some guy. What are you going to use the build the clap-o-meter out of interest? Maybe that boat in the photo? I'm sorry that I haven't sent you my photo. I'm just so worried that you won't think I am beautiful.

Bobby

From: Benjamin Suma
To: Bob Servant
Subject: Am waiting

Darling I promise, ask me anything and I will do. I do not know where wood will come from for the building but it will come. You must send the photo. I already love you in my mind and I will show my appreciation and build this thing for you. Believe me my good feeling for you is beyond explanations. I am waiting and then we need to talk about investment.

From: Bob Servant
To: Benjamin Suma
Subject: I'm scared

Benjamin,

I'm so nervous! Carol is coming round tomorrow to help with my make-up and hair for the photo. I hope you think I'm pretty! Good luck with Clap-o-Meter, it should be relatively straightforward but don't be too proud to ask for help if needed. You men are so stubborn sometimes!

Bobby x

From: Benjamin Suma
To: Bob Servant
Subject: OK

Thanks darling, am relief to read your mail. I will start to build it today. Yes you are so pretty than you might think i thought of you. I am waiting for the picture.

Benjamin

From: Bob Servant
To: Benjamin Suma
Subject: Promise

Do you promise you'll think I'm pretty?

From: Benjamin Suma
To: Bob Servant
Subject: Yes I did

YES I PROMISED YOU ARE SO PRETTY DARLING

From: Bob Servant
To: Benjamin Suma
Subject: OK HERE WE GO!

DELETE THIS AT YOUR PERIL

Ok, well here is the photo[36], I hope you like it!

Bobby x

- - - - - - - - - - - - - - - -

No Reply

---

36 This man is not Bob Servant and I have not been able to ascertain his identity. I can, however, report that he's an impressive-looking gentleman, and I really don't see what Benji's problem is.

8
Peter's Pots

From: Peter Anderson
To: Bob Servant
Subject: REPRESENTATIVE (JOB OFFER)

Dear Beloved,
Pleasant day, I have a job offer for you. My name is Peter Anderson, I am 46 years of age and I work with UNION VENTURES INC.LTD. We extract raw materials from Africa for clients in American geographical region (United States and Canada).

We are looking for a representative in America and Canada to work for us as a part time worker and are willing to Pay 10% every transaction. These payment would come to you in your name, so all you need do is cash it out, deduct your payment and wire the rest to us via Western Union. But sometimes the (FBI) gets involved incase someone tries to run with our money, I hope that is okay.

We are looking forward to your quick reply. Please if you are interested give us your full contact details

Regards,

Peter Anderson

From: Bob Servant
To: Peter Anderson
Subject: Hello there

Peter,
This sounds very interesting indeed. And thanks for the tip off about the FBI. I have long suspected they are monitoring my affairs and this just confirms it. One thing though, I'm not in America. Big Bobby comes boxing out of the badlands of Broughty Ferry,

Your Servant,

Bob Servant

From: Peter Anderson
To: Bob Servant
Subject: HI

Good day to you,
This is OK, we also need representatives where you live. The FBI would only be involved in our man runs with money. You are to work for us as our part time worker and receive payments from our customers. They pay direct into your account or send you check

138   DELETE THIS AT YOUR PERIL

which you cash and deduct your % and send to us the rest through reliable source western union money transfer. We deal in raw materials so the sums will be often large, so will your % be!

Your faithfully,

Peter Anderson.

From: Bob Servant
To: Peter Anderson
Subject: What materials Pedro? There may be a market

Hello Peter,
Good to hear from you. Can you tell me a little more please about the raw materials you deal in? I have a good friend over here – Frank Theplank - who is a trader in raw materials and I think we might be able to talk turkey.

Yours in hope,

Bob

From: Peter Anderson
To: Bob Servant
Subject: Hello Bob

HI,
Nice hearing from you. Regarding your question, Union Ventures is number one registered company in west Africa that deals on all kinds of raw materials. Still looking forward to get the informations specified, but tell us about your friend's business needs and we may be able to work with him,

Thank you.

From: Bob Servant
To: Peter Anderson
Subject: Frank's Needs

Peter
How are you my man? I'm sitting having a mug of OVD and watching Countdown. I like to call it Rum and Sums. I have just phoned Frank and told him a little bit about you. He was busy with the Coronation Street fruit machine at the Ferry Inn but he sounded quite interested

and said to ask if you deal in any of the following -

Timber
Rubber
China Pots

Look forward to hearing from you,

Bob

From: Peter Anderson
To: Bob Servant
Subject: Hello

Hi,
Bob i got your mail. Yes we deal in Timber, Rubber, China pots and many others. Please tell your friend. We are a large company and so can do discounts,

Thanks You,

Peter

From: Bob Servant
To: Peter Anderson
Subject: HE WANTS THOSE POTS

Peter,
OK, I have just called Frank. He is particularly interested in the china pots, just as I knew he would be. Frank has the Decorations Contract for a number of Dundee's parks and so pots play a major part in his life. If I was to be honest with you Peter, Frank is absolutely barmy about pots. As I suspect you might be also? Frank's going to come round here tomorrow, would you be able to send me some photos of your pots and also how much they cost?

It's bloody freezing here Peter, it's been snowing since last night. What's that all about, it's nearly summer. The Courier says it's a freak incident, though I was along at Stewpot's bar last night and the consensus there was that it's either global warming or to do with a big fire in Whitfield at the weekend.

It was the monthly animal noise competition at Stewpot's last night. I don't know why I bother because, frankly, Chappy Williams has it sown up with his chinchilla. Anyway, I came in sixth out of ten with my rhino which wasn't too bad. I have to say the big success of the night was Tommy Peanuts with a new elephant impression that

140   DELETE THIS AT YOUR PERIL

was really very good and quite scary. He wore a turban to make it an Indian elephant which everyone found very funny though I thought was a cheap trick and also you're not supposed to have props so it was a bit out of order.

I said this to Chappy in the toilets and he said that Tommy was getting a bit big for his boots so went out and built a big nob out of snow and a traffic cone on the bonnet of Tommy's car. Then Chappy said to me, 'That's a nob fit for an elephant, eh Bob?', and we both laughed even though our hands were really cold. Sometimes he's a right idiot Chappy, but every so often he comes up with a belter. I was in stitches the whole way home and the one thing I couldn't get out of my head was, 'this is the kind of thing that would crack Peter up'. Do you find it funny?

All the very best,

Many thanks,

Bob "Pots" Servant

From: Peter Anderson
To: Bob Servant
Subject: THESE ARE SOME OF OUR COMPANY SAMPLES

Bob,
Yes what your friend Chappy did was very funny to me also. I hope your bad weather has stopped. Bob, here are some of our samples. Union Ventures are ready to offer you and Frank the best products and services. We will be proud to work with you,

Peter Anderson.

From: Bob Servant
To: Peter Anderson
Subject: LOOKING GOOD

Peter,
This all looks great. I didn't realise that your company has a partnership with 'Pots a Plenty'. I think you and I both know that those cats are generally considered to be number one in terms of pots. I'll be honest with you Peter, as you have been with me, these pots look absolutely perfect and I think Frank is going to be quietly impressed. I am going to print out the photos and nip along to Doc Ferry's to catch him before he heads off. He always has to get home for Neighbours, does old Frank.

Peter, do you mind if I ask you to send a photo of yourself? I feel like we're friends and it would be good to know what you look like.

What are you up to tonight? I've got Frank coming round for a chicken party. We had six last time but then Frank was sick in my socks drawer so I think we're going to take it a bit easier tonight.

Look forward to seeing your photo and I will let you know what Frank thinks about the pots. I think he'll like them,

Bob

From: Peter Anderson
To: Bob Servant
Subject: Hello

Hello Bob,
This is my picture[37]. I am looking forward to hearing your order quickly so I can put my top boys onto the job and have it ready to go for you. Chicken is a big dish here also, it is a speciality of my wife!

Yours,

Peter

From: Bob Servant
To: Peter Anderson
Subject: Tall, Dark and Handsome too you lucky beggar!

Peter,
If you don't mind me saying you are a very, very handsome man. My God Peter, you're a sensation. Those are the most come to bed eyes

---

37 Image of an extremely dashing gentleman removed for legal reasons.

DELETE THIS AT YOUR PERIL

that I have ever seen. Forget come to bed, they're run to bed!

I finally managed to track down Frank. He'd been away playing the Cops and Robbers fruit machine at the ex-serviceman's club all day. When I found him he was lying on one of the benches on the Esplanade. He didn't make much sense but he did say that he would maybe take 500 pots from you if the price is right.I didn't tell him that you're such a big spunk though, or he might keep you for himself!

Any plans tonight? I'm just waiting for the football to come on, though some of the dross they have on the shows these days is embarrassing. Scotsport for example, that's the bloody pits. It kills me if I've not made the United game and I have to tune into that garbage to catch the highlights. Bring back Dougie Donnelly, eh[38]?

But we've got this lad at United just now Peter, called Barry Robson and that's why I can't miss the goals. He's a skinny wee ginger but, my God, the kid's got it all. The shoulder drop, the old swing of the hips. By Christ Peter, Robson could go out there in slippers and they wouldn't get near him.

Have a great night, God knows you deserve it,

Bob

From: Peter Anderson
To: Bob Servant
Subject: 500 is OK for a start

Good day Mr Bob,
I hope your team won.It is good news about the order. 500 pots would be no problem for us here and you can promise Frank that they will be put together in our best factory. We are going to give you a credit facility here at UNION VENTURES as we know that Frank is a good businessman and character. We are also going to award you a 10% discount. So all we need right now is a deposit of $20 a pot and you can pay the balance later. That is $10,000 for now.

Peter Anderson

---

38 It should be made clear that this is purely Bob's opinion on the STV weekly show *Scotsport*. Dougie Donnelly is a long-standing employee of the BBC and, as such, is unlikely to be contractually capable of taking up Bob's suggestion. Whether he would wish to do so, however, is another matter entirely.

DELETE THIS AT YOUR PERIL 143

From: Bob Servant
To: Peter Anderson
Subject: 2,000 POTS!

Peter,

I just had a quick drink with Frank at Jolly's. He was having a great run on the Andy Capp fruit machine so it was hard to get his full attention but what he did say was -

'Bob, tell your man in Africa to get the guys in for a double shift because I am ready to put in an order that will blow his socks off'.

He then said, to my utter astonishment, that he need 2,000 pots by the end of the month! He has just agreed his budget with the council for doing a major reworking of Dawson Park. They're getting rid of the tennis courts and he is going to replace it with -

'FRANK'S WORLD OF POTS'.

There are going to be 2,000 pots filled with different things. Some plants but also surprises like chocolate bars, yo-yos, jazz mags and Chinese food. Passers-by will pay £2 and put their hand in any pot they choose and see what they come up with.

It's a fantastic idea that is really going to shake things up over here. There is no doubt that this is going to take a lot of custom away from the swimming baths, the bowling club and, please God, the Limbo Walking Club who are a bunch of idiots.

It's going to be very, very interesting Peter. Certainly the swimming baths are not going to take this lying down. I wouldn't be suprised if they brought back Fancy Dress Sundays. That had them queueing right down to Youngy's Garage back when they last did it. It was a great idea and there were some wonderful scenes in the pool. I'll never forget pushing in the Queen Mother, pulling down Hitler's shorts and then dive bombing three Michael Jacksons. There's not many people that can say they've done that down the swimming baths! I'm probably the only one.

The police made them stop holding Fancy Dress Sundays after Chappy and Frank nearly drowned. How they thought they were going to swim in a donkey outfit I have no fucking idea but that's what the whole Fancy Dress Sunday scene did to people. It sent them bloody loopy. It was just a great time in Broughty Ferry's history and I really believe that FRANK'S WORLD OF POTS could have a similar effect.

Bob

From: Peter Anderson
To: Bob Servant

144  DELETE THIS AT YOUR PERIL

Subject: LOOKING FORWARD TO HEARING FROM YOU SOONEST

Hi Bob,
I am very glad to hear from you again. I think what Frank and you are to do will be a great success and I am glad UNION VENTURES will be part of this. We will be very proud.

Regarding the order it will only take us a week as we will have the whole factory working night and day on it. The final cost to you will be $39 for each pot and then the postal costs. But as I tell you, for now you pay $20 each pot as a deposit. For 2,000 pots that's $40,000. If this is a problem we can go with the agreed deposit of $10,000.

You must pay this money through Western Union so we can start on Frank's pots.

Peter

From: Bob Servant
To: Peter Anderson
Subject: Can you come?

Peter,
Frank just called me from the dog track. He said I was to make sure that the pots are suitable for people to put their hands in without risking the hands getting stuck. Most importantly, this must include motorbike riders who have not taken their gloves off because Frank says that most of those boys are fucking nutters so if their hands got stuck then they'd be liable to smash the pot over Frank's head.

Also, Frank asked if you would like to come over here with the pots. He said that you would be able to make sure they arrived safely and that you could help install the pots in Dawson Park and stay for the launch party.

What do you think? I'm not sure where you're based (Hunksville going on your photo!) but Frank says he will pay your train fare and, if it's OK with you, you can stay in my house? I just spoke to him there at The Fort where he was playing the fruit machine. I said, 'Have you won the jackpot Frank?' and he said 'I'll win the jackpot, Bob, when these fucking pots arrive'.

Bob

From: Peter Anderson
To: Bob Servant
Subject: VERY URGENT MR BOB

Mr Bob,

 To remind you we need the payment of $10,000 so we can begin. I have the factory and boys ready to go. we will need a final deposit of $40,000 for the 2,000 pots for Frank's new idea.

 It is hard for me to take too much time away from work so I am not so sure that I can come with the pots. So please make sure everything is in good position and advise me when you can make a payment.

Peter

From: Bob Servant
To: Peter Anderson
Subject: Hello Peter

Peter,
You can come?! That is great news. I am very excited and so is Frank. I just phoned him, he was driving back from the casino but he shouted 'That's great news Bob, tell Peter I can't wait to meet him and his pots but if the pots are no good I'll shove them up his' before he got cut off by the Tannadice tunnel.

 Peter, I would like to take this opportunity to formally invite you to stay at my house. I have attached a photo. I don't know if it's the kind of set-up you'll be used to but the one thing I can guarantee is 'fun'.

 I can't wait to see you and the pots. Peter and his magnificent pots. Potty Peter. Peter Pots.

Bob

DELETE THIS AT YOUR PERIL

From: Peter Anderson
To: Bob Servant
Subject: Re: Hello Peter

Hello Bob,
I'm happy as well receiving your mail, how is your business and
Frank hope everything is good. Well OK then Bob I will come with
the pots. It is a nice offer that you have made and your house looks
nice. I will come by plane with the pots and I know the airline
through business so I will not have to buy a ticket.
    Bob I advise you to send the $10,000 by Western Union or by
money gramm money transfer. Here is company cashier information
to use

Name: ▄▄▄▄▄▄▄▄▄▄▄
City :Lagos
Test Qestion: From
Answer : Bob

Thanks,

Peter Anderson.

From: Bob Servant
To: Peter Anderson
Subject: HUNKY PETER'S BIG WEEK WITH BOB AND FRANK

Hi Peter,
I'm just trying to knock out the plan for your trip here. Have a little
look at it. It's only a rough draft so if there's anything you're not
happy with let me know.

DAY ONE

Peter arrives. A day of relaxation where Peter is left to chill out and
have naps. Bob occasionally pops into his room to see if he's OK. If
he wants then Bob could massage his feet, or bring him snacks. In
the evening Frank comes round to the house and they all get to
know each other. We have a light dinner of fritter rolls from
Maciocia's chip shop and then retire to the jacuzzi with some
Ribena, a large trifle and over 400 jazz mags.

DAY TWO

Time to get 'potty'. Peter, Frank and Bob go to Dawson Park and
oversee the installation of the pots. Peter checks the pots and

DELETE THIS AT YOUR PERIL   147

makes sure they aren't damaged. Bob and Frank watch him closely, not because they suspect he is up to no good but because they will be admiring a man at the top of his game, doing the thing he loves. Peter then gives Bob and Frank a brief description of the pots, what they like and don't like, and the best way of looking after them. Peter then joins Frank, Bob, Chappy Williams and Tommy Peanuts for a curry at the Gullistan. Chappy to do the toast and Tommy to do the after-dinner speech as long he promises not to make fun of Bob because it's him that has set the whole thing up.

DAY THREE

Peter and Bob go on a daytrip to the Camperdown Zoo. Bob makes sandwiches, Peter to choose filling. If it's sunny we have a picnic, if it's raining we will eat the food under one of the wooden ships. We talk about parks and funny things that have happened to us in parks.

DAY FOUR

Potty Peter's Media blitz. Peter is guest on Radio Tay's breakfast show where he tells funny stories about pots and about how Bob is a good guy. He then goes into town (taxi with Bob, the two of them to go halfers on the fare) where he does interviews for the Dundee Courier and the Evening Telegraph. During the Evening Telegraph interview Peter lets slip that he has new evidence that strongly suggests a group of gypsies stole Bob's ladders in 1996.

DAY FIVE

Final preparations. Peter, Bob and Frank go up to Dawson Park, roll their sleeves up and make any last minute adjustments needed. Then some role play, with Peter pretending to be a passer-by and testing the various pots to make sure his hand doesn't get stuck in any of them. Peter to check every single pot and then to do so again wearing a glove. Bob and Frank to wait for him in the beer garden at the Taychreggan Hotel next to the park. Bob and Frank to give Peter a torch in case it gets dark before he's finished.

DAY SIX

Launch Day! Party, Party, Party. Bob to wake Peter up with a bacon roll and small glass of sherry to get him in the zone then we're off up to Dawson Park to get ready for the crowds and support Frank. When the crowds come, Bob and Peter to control the pots, checking everyone is happy and using the pots correctly. Then Frank to give a

  **DELETE THIS AT YOUR PERIL**

speech in which he mentions Bob and Peter and clearly notes the work that both have put in. Peter to then make a short speech including some jokes but mostly serious and talking about the pots and what they have been through to be with us in Dawson Park. Bob to then make a short speech that brings the house down.

DAY SEVEN

The blow out. Bob, Peter, Frank, Chappy and Tommy to go out on the town. Bob and Peter to wear matching denim and casual jackets and to spend most of the night together. Bob to get women over and Peter to tell them interesting stories and jokes and also to tell them that Bob is a great guy and to mention about how Bob is worth a few quid but doesn't like to talk about it.

DAY EIGHT

Peter leaves first thing for the airport with Frank driving him. Bob to come only if head not too sore.

What do you think Peter, all OK?

From: Peter Anderson
To: Bob Servant
Subject: OK apart from second last!

Hello Bob,
Yes this all looks fine and I think we will have a lot of fun as well as working hard to make success. Please speak to Frank and get the money so we can get started and make this great dream of ours a reality. There is only one problem with your plan Bob because I am married as I have told you and do not participate in women affairs thank you. Otherwise I am looking forward to hear from you soonest.

From: Bob Servant
To: Peter Anderson
Subject: Hook a brother up?

Peter,
Give me a break here. I am a single guy and am constantly looking for skirt. There are a lot of opportunities for this in Broughty Ferry, more than you'd think. There's the bowling club coffee morning on a Tuesday and the fortnightly Car Boot Sale on the Esplanade. Of course, the big one is the Limbo Walking Club's Annual Walk-Off but

I picked up a lifetime ban from that lot over the whole 2002 clean-up campaign mix-up[39].

I need a wingman Peter and I thought that you could be that guy. You're a handsome devil and I know that the birds here would think you were a right James Bond with all your foreign travel and stuff. Christ, you should have seen when Chappy Williams came back from seeing his brother in Australia. The birds threw themselves at him, it was like he was Christopher Fucking Columbus when, in actual fact, he'd got the tickets free with his Hoover.

Are you up for hitting the town when you're here and we can see if our luck's in? I bet you're a confident bugger. Also, what kind of food do you like?

Thanks,

Bob

From: Peter Anderson
To: Bob Servant
Subject: OK

Bob,
If it is a party then of course I will talk to women and if it helps you out then better for all. Regarding food there is an old adage that says when in Rome you do as Romans do, as for me i like what ever that will be good for Bob.

Now please Bob, do you have the money to send by Western Union? The boys are waiting to start but I can not keep them from other jobs for long?

Peter

From: Bob Servant
To: Peter Anderson
Subject: Book

---

39 The *Broughty Ferry Gazette* of 27 March 2002 carried a headline of 'Limbo Walking Club Treasurer in Embezzlement Outrage' and included a suggestion from a Mr Robert Servant (48) that he had seen Hamish Instrell, the treasurer of the local Limbo Walking Club, drinking cocktails in the West Indies on a television documentary just days after the Club had reported it was in a financial crisis after poor T-shirt sales. The *Broughty Ferry Gazette* of 28 March 2002 carried a full-page apology to the Limbo Walking Club and Mr Instrell that included a report that a Mr Robert Servant (57) had in fact been watching the feature film 'Cocktail' whilst heavily inebriated and mistook one of the film's actors for Mr Instrell.

  **DELETE THIS AT YOUR PERIL**

Peter,
A strange thing has happened. I got talking to this kid. He's a weird one, I used to go to his house to do his windows and I sometimes see him skulking about the pubs and so on. Anyway, turns out he's a writer and he reckons that there could be something in all this emailing that I've been doing. He's been going through it all and thinks he's going to stick the whole lot in a bloody book and get in the shops and so on.

What do you think? Sounds a bit dodgy to me,

Bob

From: Peter Anderson
To: Bob Servant
Subject: Western Union

Bob,
YOU MUST GO TO WESTERN UNION. Yes books are great things but we must concentrate on the matter in hand.

From: Bob Servant
To: Peter Anderson
Subject: It's Goodbye from Bobby Boy

Peter.
Or I could be saying Jack, or Jean, Alexandra, Colin, Joseph, Benjamin or so many, many others. My God Peter I've had some fun. It's only now, when this kid Forsyth's been here and poking through my stuff that I can see how long I've been writing to you lot. It seems like yesterday that I nearly got hold of some golden lions, but turns out I've been messing about with you boys for months and months. I can't really remember a lot of it if I'm honest with you, just that we chatted about the Ferry and Frank and the rest of the lads.

But anyway, he reckons that he has enough for the book and I should stop now for the sake of my mental health. He says he's going to take me up to Doc Ferry's and get the drinks in but I think he's one of those boys that gives it that and then suddenly his pockets are superglued after two rounds[40].

---

40 For the record, on that particular evening I bought Bob eight drinks, lent him £5 for a kebab and bought two pornographic magazines at his request from the Shell Garage in Broughty Ferry.

I suppose we'll just have to see how we go. Good luck my friend, and if you see any of the rest of them tell them old Bobby Boy passes on his best. Tell them it was just a bit of fun, something to wrap up the nights. Christ only knows, the nights get long.

Sleep tight my friend, keep smiling.

Your Servant,

Bob Servant.

From: Peter Anderson
To: Bob Servant
Subject: LAST CHANCE

Bob,
Do you want the pots or not? I need an answer now. I will wait for an hour and then you will missed your chance.

No Reply

DELETE THIS AT YOUR PERIL

Acknowledgements

Thanks to David Riding and all at MBA, Natasha Martin and all at Aurum, to those who generously allowed me to use their images in such absurd ways – Dennis Cox, Tony Northrup, Ansa Bulfone, Marion Boddy-Evans, Tom Nardone, Jane Tonnfeldt, Dundee United, Jayne Cremasco and Joie Leung – and as always to my family, Jane and my pals. And to old men in bars.

And now to Bob. I have been trying for the last week to ascertain if he wished to thank anyone and it's turned into a torturous task, which peaked in intensity yesterday. A regrettable run of events commenced in mid-morning, when Bob called, in fine form I should say, to give me three names: Tommy Peanuts, Chappy Williams and Frank The Plank (otherwise known as Frank Theplank).

'They're my best mates,' he explained, 'And they deserve everything they get.'

In the three went, only for Bob to call in the early afternoon from Broughty Ferry, absolutely furious. Chappy Williams had just played a cruel joke on him in Stewpot's bar, swapping the salt in the shaker on Bob's table for sugar and allowing Bob to apply a typically liberal dose to his scampi and chips.

'I knew something was wrong straight away,' Bob revealed as he waited patiently at the Gray Street level crossing, 'but I kept my dignity and ate the whole lot. I was going to try and say something to Chappy about being sweet enough already but I just left it and I'm going home with my head held high. But I want him out right now Neil, right bloody now.'

I accepted Bob's decision without question and all was quiet until dinnertime, when Bob called again. There was a distinctive echo and he disclosed that he was calling from a toilet cubicle at Doc Ferry's bar.

'Take Tommy out,' he whispered urgently, 'he just pulled away my stool as I went to sit down with a couple of birds. I looked like a fucking idiot and I've got a really sore back.'

So we were down to Frank The Plank. But, less than an hour later, Bob was on the phone again. Frank was also to be ejected, he declared, as he had just looked out of the window at Doc Ferry's and spotted Frank wearing Bob's favourite jumper on a passing bus.

'I said he could have it for a week for his birthday,' Bob told me gravely, 'but that was nearly a month ago.'

At this point I was under pressure, with the book's text needing to be submitted first thing this morning to the printer's. And so it was with some consternation that I received a stream of calls from Bob last night. I loyally noted each in turn, and here they are:

8.25pm. Bob calls to say that Tommy Peanuts, Chappy Williams and Frank The Plank are all to be immediately reinstated in the book's acknowledgement section after the four gather in Doc Ferry's bar and are 'getting on great guns'.

8.27pm. Bob calls to request Tommy Peanuts be removed from the book's acknowledgement section with immediate effect after Tommy comments twice within a minute that Bob's hair 'looks like women's hair'.

9.26pm. Bob calls to request Chappy Williams be removed from the book's acknowledgement section with immediate effect. Chappy told Bob that a man who entered the bar was his friend Dave and that Bob would like him and should go and say hello. When Bob approached the man and introduced himself he quickly realised that Chappy did not know the man and the man was not called Dave. Chappy had fabricated both facts for his own amusement, and also that of Tommy Peanuts and Frank The Plank.

10.36pm. Bob calls to request Frank The Plank be removed from the book's acknowledgement section with immediate effect. Apparently Frank is still wearing Bob's jumper. 'I knew something was up,' says Bob, 'because he's had his jacket on all night and has been sweating like something else. I caught him outside with his jacket unzipped and fanning himself with the lunch menu. The guy's a snake.'

11.10pm. Bob calls to request Tommy Peanuts, Chappy Williams and Frank The Plank be reinstated in the book's acknowledgement section with immediate effect after the three surprise Bob with the gift of a special chocolate cigar.

11.12pm. Bob calls to firmly request that Tommy Peanuts, Chappy Williams and Frank The Plank be removed from the book's acknowledgement section with immediate effect. He is phoning once again from the toilet cubicle and, in the midst of a disconcert-ing gagging sequence, reveals that the chocolate cigar was just a normal cigar that Tommy had placed in a used Mars Bar wrapper.

It was during this final call that Bob made a startling announcement.
    'They're all bastards, Neil,' he shouted, his voice reverberating sternly amongst the tiling. 'And I want you to write that.'
    'Are you sure Bob?' I asked politely. 'That'll be the end of the book.'

'Do it,' he said, quieter and with magnificent poise, before the gagging returned and the phone died.

So there you go – that is that, the end.

They're all bastards.

Neil Forsyth

London, July 2007